Accurate Weather Predictions
With Deep Learning

by

Uma Sharma

LIST OF TABLES

LIST OF FIGURES

LIST OF ABBREVIATIONS

AI	Artificial Intelligence
AIC	Akaike's Information Criteria
ANFIS	Adaptive Neuro Fuzzy Inference System
ANN	Artificial Neural Network
AR	Auto Regressive
ARIMA	Auto Regressive Integrated Moving Average
ARMA	Auto Regressive Moving Average
ARX	Auto Regressive Exogenous
AWS	Automatic Weather Stations
Bi-LSTM	Bidirectional Long Short-Term Memory
BMA	Bayesian Model Averaging
BPTT	Back Propagation Through Time
CNN	Convolutional Neural Networks
CRBM	Conditional Restricted Boltzmann Machine
CRNN	Convolutional Recurrent Neural Network
CWDS	Cyclone Warning Dissemination System
DBL	Deep Belief Networks
DL	Deep Learning
DLWP	Deep Learning-based Weather Prediction
FFNN	Feed Forward Neural Network
GPU	Graphical Processing Unit
LR	Learning Rate
LSTM	Long Short Term Memory
MAE	Mean absolute Error
MIMO	Multi Input Multi Output
MISO	Multi Input Single Output
ML	Machine Learning
MLR	Multiple Linear Regression
MSE	Mean Square Error
NWP	Numerical Weather Prediction

PBL	Planetary Boundary Layer
PNN	Probability Neural Network
RF	Random Forest
RMSE	Root Mean Square Error
RNN	Recurrent Neural Network
RNN	Recurrent Neural Network
SGD	Stochastic Gradient Descent
SISO	Single Input Single Output
SNN	Shared Nearest Neighbour
SVM	Support Vector Machine
TCN	Temporal Convolutional Networks
WPS	Weather Processing System
WRF	Weather Research Forecasting

TABLE OF CONTENTS

CHAPTER-1

INTRODUCTION

Chapter 1

Introduction

In earlier days, observing the sky was the first step in forecasting, which was supplemented by the invention of weather forecasting instruments like Hygrometer, Thermometer, and Anemometer etc. [1]. Observing techniques and forecasting devices have developed to the state of art in recent years and launching exclusive Meteorological satellites [2] and Radars has now made possible to monitor the weather closely and accurately. In today's fast telecommunication network, countries exchange weather observations and updates rapidly through the help of Meteorological satellites to produce near accurate predictions [3]. Apart from various Government organizations and the weather observatory stations, many private agencies have evolved to make predictions on the weather and this information are shared through the latest smart devices is a good sign indicating the growth and the development of Weather Forecasting and its technologies.

This Chapter discusses about Meteorology [4], its applications, Weather Forecasting [5], Traditional Weather Forecasting methods, Forecasting Devices and Existing Models. The chapter also focuses on the importance and the need for Weather Forecasting, along with objectives of our proposed work and also highlights the social significance of this research work.

1.1 Meteorology

Meteorology is the science of weather, in broad terms, it is the study of the atmosphere [6] and is an integrated system constituting atmosphere, land and ocean [7].The meteorology word comes from the Greek word called "meteoron" referring to any phenomenon related to the sky [8]. Observing, understanding and interpretation of weather are the three basic aspects of meteorology [9][10][11].Weather observations are carried out through simple instruments like the thermometer [12], anemometer [13] and are plotted on weather charts to be analyzed by meteorologists at Weather stations. Recent advances in modern computers, supercomputers, radars and satellites [12] have resulted in the noteworthy progress in the meteorology field

1

[14]. Weather and climate related changes have direct or indirect affect on most of the economic, industrial, agricultural, social, commercial, transport related processes. The atmosphere is affected and sustained upon lives of people, animals, pests, insects and microorganisms, plants, trees, forests and marine life in their life cycle of growth and development [15][16][17]. Meteorology, therefore, shows a major part in all facets of modern human life. The Applications of Meteorology [18] are enormous and a few are listed below:

- Weather forecasting
- Aviation meteorology
- Agricultural meteorology
- Hydro meteorology
- Military meteorology
- Nuclear meteorology
- Maritime meteorology

The Job of Weather forecasters differs like,

- An operational forecaster analyzes and issues day to day forecasts.
- A research meteorologist on disastrous events like earthquakes, tsunamis, landslide, flash flood and erratic climate changes.
- In military, for safety and security of the nation.
- Airlines, updates the pilots about the weather status on take-off, land in and in between.
- In Agriculture, for the cultivation of crops, meteorology plays a vital role in crop production, the right period for sowing, in determining soil moisture, and migration of pests etc.

Thus, Meteorology and Weather forecasting are closely related and serves the mankind and all living beings for its existence and survival on this planet Earth. This made us to draw to the conclusion of using Data Mining Techniques [19] for weather forecasting.

1.2 Weather Forecasting

Weather Forecasting is high in complexity, multidimensional and a dynamic method [20] as it includes a number of entities related to atmosphere along with various theories of mathematics, thermodynamics, atmospheric physics, laws of motion, conservation of energy, etc. So, meteorologists are continuously making efforts for upgrading the forecasts related accuracy in spite of the sudden changes leading to difficulty in predicting weather patterns and climate changes occurring worldwide due to global warming [21]. Hence, Atmospheric Studies [22] and Weather forecasting is being a continuous, updating and challenging phenomenon in today's world [23].

Weather Forecasting is referred to as forecasting the forthcoming weather conditions depending upon the historical data collection [24]. It is one of the vital applications of Meteorology. Weather and Climate are the measures of time [25]. Weather is the atmosphere's condition during a shorter period of time, whereas, Climate is the behavior of the atmosphere during the longer duration [26]. Out of several meteorological elements major components, namely temperature, pressure, wind, humidity, and precipitation has a significant impact in shaping the weather and the climate of a place [27]. Analysis of these meteorological elements forms the basis for forecasting the weather and to determine the climate of a location [28].

As a result of depending upon the number of factors, the procedure of weather related predictions becomes complex and challenging as well [29]. Fluctuations in weather conditions are noticed every few hours and extreme changes occur from time to time [30]. Being aware about the weather conditions earlier itself leads to reduction in the losses, helping us in numerous ways. Weather forecasting has wider applications varying from being useful for a student to keep an umbrella when being aware that it would rain in the evening to being useful for governmental establishments in emptying a locality when being aware about the possibility of heavy rain in that area. Forecasting is the undertaking of expectation of the environment at a future time and a given zone [31]. In the early days, this has been completed through physical conditions in which the air is considered as runny. The present condition of the earth is studied, and the future phase is anticipated through unraveling those conditions arithmetically, yet we cannot decide an exact climate for beyond what days and this can be improved with the assistance of science and innovation [32].

Weather Forecasting is a process of distinguishing and foreseeing to a precise exactness of climatic conditions by the usage of a number of innovations. Generally, different procedures were utilized to foresee the climate, in view of perception of

3

ecological and meteorological components, for example, sunlight, clouds and animal conduct. These predictions were not frequently logical or precise.

Climate estimates are made by gathering the most extreme measure of information conceivable about the current scenario of the environment (specifically humidity, temperature, and wind speed) and the usage of comprehension of barometrical processes in deciding that how the atmospheric changes takes place later. In this century, it is one of the most experimented and mechanically tested issue remaining so far globally. This is predictable principally to two variables: first, it's utilized for some human exercises and moreover, due to the advantage made by the various mechanical advances which are justifiably identified by this solid research field, likely to the progress of calculation and the enhancement in estimation frameworks. Making a precise forecast is becoming one of the significant difficulties confronting meteorologist everywhere globally. Climate prediction is one of the most intriguing and entrancing area since ancient times [33]. Researchers have made attempts in finding out the meteorological qualities by the use of many techniques, a part of these strategies being more accurate than the other ones [34].

Weather prediction is attracting the enthusiasm of the exploration network, for the most part on account of its impact on human life. An earlier admonition for potential atmosphere calamities may possibly several numbers of lives throughout the years to come [35]. The capability of the climate prediction has been demonstrating its value in the horticultural division like arranging ranch tasks, for example, stockpiling and transportation of nourishment grains. Earlier data of cyclones and heavy rainfalls are vital for the security and insurance of human life [36]. It further aides in diminishing the harm acquired as a national loss. Extremely worst climate condition likewise hampers the transportation and administration division truly, causing an expansion of dangers like mishaps, and postponement in the offered administration just as the nature of service.

The procedure of weather forecasting is fundamentally reliant on model-based techniques like recreating dynamical frameworks by using the intensity of a fractional differential equation [37].The Numerical expectation of a climate gauge utilizes computational models [38] planned based on notable physical standards related with seas [39] and air, to improve the estimation of future environmental conditions, in

4

view of the present climate and other influencing parameters. The environment can be demonstrated like a liquid. The present atmospheric state can be examined, and the forthcoming state will be looked like by getting the arrangement of liquid elements and thermodynamics conditions. Quantitative estimate such as humidity, rainfall and temperature are proved to be significant in the horticulture zone, just like merchants inside product markets [40][41]. These days, we are utilizing numerous methodologies for climate estimation [42]. Statistical modelling, Mathematical modelling and Artificial Intelligence strategies are some of them [43]. Mathematical modelling of the climate to foresee future climate dependent on current climate conditions is numerical climate prediction. It needs full information of atmospheric elements and includes estimation with countless factors and datasets [44].

The traditionally used weather forecast procedures that used satellite images and weather stations are costly due to the inclusion of processes being high in cost and complexity both [45]. Weather forecast by the use of machine learning is low in cost, takes lesser time, higher in convenience, real in time and precise in nature [37]. A few of the present researches related to weather forecasting including machine learning technique involved the usage of much of the former weather data [46]. The accuracy of the forecasts depends upon the models being trained with. Thus, it becomes much essential for any machine learning model to be trained with a highly precise data. The data attained from a number of sources is not trustworthy all the time. Thus, it becomes necessary to preprocess the data. Preprocessing of the data includes the removal of needless columns that are not relevant to the model's forecast, removal of the zero values, merging the same columns and various other stages related to pre-processing [47].

Machine Learning is generally strong to annoyances and doesn't require some other physical factors for expectation. Hence, AI is greatly improved open door in advancement of climate estimation [48]. Prior to the progression of Technology, climate estimation was a hard nut to separate. Climate forecasters depended upon satellites, information model's environmental conditions with less precision. Climate forecast and investigation has inconceivably expanded regarding exactness and consistency with the utilization of Internet of Things since most recent years. Using the intensity of strategies identified with AI, and to give a superior and proficient arrangement of this information requesting test, which contains derivations over the existence, has acquired a huge measure of consideration of the specialists in the last decade [49]. While contrasting, numerical forecast of climate, focal point of information driven methodologies is for using authentic climate information for the preparation of AI models. The AI models, as a rule, have two kinds of design, shallow and deep. The shallow AI strategies centers on dealing with crude information and the expert of this area is basically required in the change of un-important information into significant portrayals. Though, deep learning based models have been altering different application spaces, promoting range from sound-related to vision signal preparing. The key bit of leeway of deep learning based strategies is that they have the ability to build claim highlights, during the preparation period of a model. It is very attractive to chop down the prerequisite of any area mastery for preparing an exact model [50].

1.2.1. Importance of Weather Forecasting

The beginning of weather forecasting started from the early civilizations and was dependent upon the observation of reoccurrence of the astronomical and meteorological processes. Presently, weather forecasts depend upon the collection of data related to the atmosphere's present state and the usage of scientific processes in predicting the further evolution of atmosphere. The disordered atmosphere's nature and the immense computational power essential for solving the overall equations describing the atmosphere leads to decrease in the accuracy of the weather predictions and also becomes costly with the rise in the range of these predictions. This makes us in brainstorming more novel processes for weather forecasting being less costly and/or more efficient.

So, forecasting the weather is being a challenging and complex process for researchers, demands a heterogeneous combination of expertise, observations, and techniques adopted from multiple disciplines. Weather on the way is important to many people. For example, farmers plan their seeding, planting, watering and harvesting schedules based on the upcoming weather [51].The Aviation department decides their flight take off, landing, flying based on the weather report[52].Tournaments[53], Big events, Series matches depends on weather schedule before fixing the dates[54] and for a common man, in his daily day to day events. It is significant for so many reasons like,

- Agriculture and Crop production
- Cultivation, sowing, weeding, harvesting
- Aviation
- Water Transport
- Marine and Sea Food
- Fisheries
- Irrigation
- Hydro power projects
- Military operations
- Natural disasters
- Storage of food grains
- Protection of livestock

1.2.2. Traditional Weather Forecasting

Human beings started to predict the weather informally over stone ages, and formally from the nineteenth century. The art of forecasting weather was started with the very early civilizations and it was based on the various astronomical phenomenon, meteorological events eventually assist them to track the seasonal variation in the weather [55]. Throughout the centuries, people made forecasts based on their weather knowledge and personal expertise [56]. By the end of the renaissance, it became the order of the day for more advanced knowledge that led to the inventions of various weather instruments.

Weather instruments were invented to measure the properties of moisture, temperature [57], wind speed [58], direction and pressure. The meteorological instruments were improved and refined through the centuries, and developments based on observational, theoretical, and technological aspects also contributed to the knowledge of the atmosphere [59].

I. Looking at the Sky:

In ancient times, the weather was predicted by observing the sky conditions. In 650 BC, Babylonians started weather prediction by close observation of the sky and the clouds [60] then after in 340 BC, Aristotle, Greek philosopher wrote a book "Meteorological" about the formation of clouds, rain, wind and thunder storm [61].

7

II. Use of Various Instruments:

The growth of science, in all domains paved the way for the long and rich history of developments of weather instruments too [62]. The advent of weather instruments namely thermometer, hygrometer, barometer, anemometer etc. helped to lay down the framework for modern astronomy, meteorology and in turn weather forecasting [63]. Nicholas Cusa, the German scientist started using hygrometer to measure the humidity of air during 1401-1464. Condensation and evaporation produce water vapour in the atmosphere, which is measured as humidity. It can be measured as either absolute or relative humidity. Galileo Galilei, an Italian scientist started using thermometer to measure the temperature during 1564-1642 [64]. After that during 1608- 1647, Evangelista Torricelli, an Italian scientist started using barometer for measuring atmospheric pressure [65]. Weather stations were equipped with these different weather instruments to observe the sky and the atmosphere and thus the weather data were accumulated for further processing [66]. In addition, scientists launch weather balloons and satellites to collect data from the atmosphere. In 1450, Leon Battista Alberti invented the anemometer, which is used for wind speed measurement, and in 1846, cup anemometer was invented by Dr. J.T.R. Robinson invented the cup anemometer. In the 1960s and 1970s,anemometers used lasers or sonars to measure wind speed [67].

III. Analog Technique:

It is a composite technique, requiring the forecaster to call upon the past climate conditions for making an assumption. It is a helpful technique for watching precipitation in spots, for example, seas, just as the determining of precipitation sums and conveyance later on. A comparative procedure is utilized in medium range estimating, which is known as teleconnections, when the frameworks in different regions are used to assist pin with the use of the area of another framework by bringing down inside the encompassing system.

IV. Ensemble Forecasting:

Meteorologists have created barometrical models to predict the atmospheric conditions by utilizing group estimating to depict how air temperature, weight and humidity will change after some time. The conditions are customized into a computing machine and the information on the present climatic conditions is

8

sustained into it. The machine analyses the circumstances to determine how the many atmospheric factors will change over the next several moments. The machine repeats this process, this time using the yield from the previous cycle as a contribution to the next cycle. The computing machine outputs its predetermined data at a later period.

V.   Radar:

After World War II , the usage of meteorological radars comes in existence to locate precipitation, calculate its motion, and estimate its type [68]. Radio Detection and Ranging is what Radar stands for. A transmitter transmits radio waves in radar. Radio waves locate the nearest item and then return to a receiver. Climate radar can detect a wide range of precipitation characteristics, including area, movement, force, and the likelihood of future precipitation [69]. The most common type of climatic radar is Doppler radar, which can also track the rate at which precipitation falls [70].

VI.   Weather Satellites:

Climate satellites have become increasingly important sources of climate information [71] since the first was propelled in 1952 and in 1960's first meteorological satellites named Tiros I was launched. Climate satellites are the most ideal approach to compute the weather conditions, similar to storms, volcanic ejection, and contamination. They can record long duration changes. In the electro-magnetic range climate satellites may watch all vitalities from all wavelengths range. Most considerable are the obvious light and the heat (infrared) frequencies [12].

These are of two types, first is Polar Orbiting Satellites which are launched parallel to the meridian lines and orbiting over the north to the south poles on each Earth's revolution, also helps in capturing the images perfectly and second is Geostationary Satellites which orbits the equator with the same speed as that of the earth, in a geosynchronous orbit enabling for continuous monitoring of a specific region, especially useful for the prediction of Storm, as it constantly watches and observes over a period of time [72].

VII.   Weather Maps:

Weather maps are visual representations of weather conditions in the environment.. Climate maps may demonstrate just one component of the air or numerous highlights.

9

They can use data from mechanical models or from human perceptions. Climate maps are mostly found in papers and on the Internet [73].

On a climate map, significant meteorological conditions will be represented for each climate station. Tides, flow of environment, dew point, overcast spread, temperature and wind speed are all factors to consider. On a climate map, meteorologists utilize a wide range of descriptions. These images give them a speedy and simple approach to put data onto the guide.

VIII. Latest Devices and Technologies:

Apart from the aforementioned weather forecasting instruments, today's weather prediction [74] procedures are being automated, by using various tools and devices such as Weather Research and Forecasting (WRF) [75], , Weather Processing System (WPS), Advanced Research WRF (ARW), Numerical Weather Prediction (NWP) Models, Doppler Weather Radars [76], Storm / Cyclone Detection Radars, and Cyclone warning dissemination system (CWDS) [77]. Also, the installation of many Weather observatory centers and Automatic weather stations (AWS) has been done.

1.3 Classification of Weather Forecasting

Every weather forecast can be characterized based on following measures:
- Temporal range of validity after emission
- Dominant technology
- Characteristics of input and output time and space resolution
- Accuracy
- Broadcasting needs

Weather is one of the significant factor of our lives, and it tends to be alluded as the one that can't be controlled whereas climate all the more regularly controls how and what individuals do that is the place we live, what we wear, and even what we eat. It is made out of the parameters like breeze, deceivability, precipitation, downpour, day off, cloud, weight and stickiness. Climate marvels for the most part occur in the lower some portion of air that is troposphere [78] which fundamentally happens because of the pneumatic force, temperature and dampness contrasts between to each other. These distinctions are caused seen because of the point of the sun that fluctuates with

10

the scope. The polar and tropical zones shift generally in temperature and this wide temperature differentiate prompted barometrical courses. Emergent upon the period, forecasting is sorted into five kinds that are given below:

Now Casting:
This type of forecasting gives details of the present weather and forecasts up to 3-4 hours ahead (less than 24 hours) [79]. It uses observational data and extrapolates the information using the latest results of numerical weather prediction (NWP) models into the future [80][79].

Short Range Forecasting:
This is the estimation of climate conditions on a regular routine that roughly predicts for one to seven days [81]. Predictions are based on satellite pictures, maps climate outlines. In this type of forecasting, constant and progression techniques are utilized. In everyday life, short range climate forecasting assumes a significant job in transportation [82].

Medium Range Forecasting:
Forecast of climate conditions around one day to one month ahead of time[83]. Medium range climate forecasting is made by the computations done by considering significant time span of climate conditions [84]. It is done by the worldwide environmental models which is dependent on deterministic techniques [85].

Long Range Forecasting:
Widen the range for estimation and spread periods between one month and a year ahead of time [86]. Long range estimates are produced using fortnight to the period of a year ahead of time [87]. It doesn't contain itemized data and has least exactness. It has utility during warmth and cold waves and during dry seasons [88].

Hazardous Weather Forecasting:
Climate risks are compromising climate events that are hazardous to life and properties [89]. Climate dangers can resemble tornadoes, lightning, tempest, hails, streak flooding and so forth [90]. The National climate administration has named

dangerous climate viewpoint, a sort of articulation that is given so as to give data of perilous or extreme climate occasions coming up inside seven days.

1.4 General Methods of Weather Forecasting

The most common types of weather forecasting methods are classified into four types, namely persistence method, physical method, statistical method (time series and ANN), and hybrid methods.

1.4.1. Persistence Method (or) Naive Predictor

A persistence method is a simplest and most economical method to forecast the weather. This approach is based on the assumptions that present and future temperature values are strongly correlated [91]. If P(t) is the observed temperature on time (t), then the expected temperature at t+ Δt could be expressed as a linear equation and is as follows:

$$P(t + \Delta t) = P(t) \qquad (1.1)$$

The linear equation above shows that temperature at time 't+ Δt' is supposed to be the same as 't' at time. For very short-term temperature forecasting, this approach is more precise than the most physical and statistical approaches. Hence, for new forecasting techniques should be tested against persistence method to validate the performance of this technique.

Limitation of the persistence method is that if the forecasting lead time gets increased the accuracy of this method gets decreased [92].

1.4.2. Physical Method

The physical approach models are the dynamics of the atmosphere, parameterized by the Planetary Boundary Layer (PBL) theory, also recognized as the Atmospheric Boundary Layer (ABL) [93]. The lowest portion of the atmosphere that is in continual contact with the earth's surface is ABL. Here, the physical numbers are turbulent and vertical mixing is higher, such as wind/air velocity, temperature, and moisture. The physical techniques consist

of certain physical equations to translate meteorological data from a certain time to temperature forecasts at a location considered. For long-term forecasting, this approach is more efficient and reliable. Numerical Weather Prediction Method (NWP) is a type of Physical method.

Numerical Weather Prediction Method (NWP)
The atmosphere is stimulated by the numerical weather forecast model by the numerical integration of motion equation beginning from the present atmospheric conditions. Numerical Weather Prediction (NWP) is based on a physical equation that uses a variety of weather parameters to solve a complex mathematical equation. The Fifth Generation Mesoscale Mode (MM5), Regional Spectra Model (RSM), Weather Research and Forecasting (WRF) model, Prediktor, HIRLAM, etc. are some of the NWP models.

The limitations of NWP model is that it is complex, expensive, limited observation set for calibration and takes high computational time.

1.4.3. Statistical Method

Based on training the model using a required sample of real data unique to that area, a statistical approach is applied, taking a number of discrete periodic cycles. The mathematical approach is based on training the model and uses the difference between the predicted values and the real immediate values to change the model parameters to minimize the forecast error. For short and medium term temperature forecasting, this approach is efficient and most reliable.

Limitation of the statistical method is that as the forecasting time increases the forecasting error also increases. Despite this limitation, this method is very simple, low cost and any stages of modeling are possible. This method is based on patterns rather than the predefined mathematical model.

The statistical method is further divided into two subdivisions:
(i) Time Series methods
(ii) Artificial Neural Network models.

    (i)   Time Series Method
The method of the Time Series attempts to model the stochastic mechanism that generates the structure of an observable series of events that are observed at certain intervals and to render future predictions via the observational values belonging to the

13

previous interval. Time Series method does not require any records beyond historical wind data. This method accurately provides the timely forecasting, and it is easy to model. Some models of Time Series method are Auto Regressive (AR), Auto Regressive Exogenous (ARX), ARMA with Exogenous inputs (ARMAX), Auto Regressive Integrated Moving Average (ARIMA), Auto Regressive Moving Average (ARMA), Grey Predictor, Linear Predictor, Algebraic Curve Fitting (ACF), Exponential Smoothing, and Bayesian Model Averaging (BMA).

Limitation of the time series method is that it cannot forecast more than a day ahead.

(ii)   Artificial Neural Network (ANN) Models

Artificial Neural Network is one of the analysis paradigms that are roughly modeled after the massive study on parallel structure of the brain. Artificial Neural Network (ANN) deals with the nonlinear and complex problem in terms of classification (or) prediction. ANN has an ability to perform nonlinear and complex modeling without a prior knowledge of the relationship between input and variables. Based on previous temperature measurement data taken for a long period of time, ANN is trained to learn the relationship between input data and temperature output.

ANN has strong self-learning ability, fault tolerance ability, real-time operation, adaptability, and cost-effectiveness (To learn the relationship of any mathematical formulation between inputs and outputs).

Few types of ANN methods are feed-forward (BPN, MLP, RBFN), Feedback (ELMAN, Recurrent), Support Vector Machine (SVM), ADALINE, Probability Neural Network (PNN), and so on.

The limitations of ANN method includes, falling into local minimum, slow convergence, difficult to confirm the structure of a network (or) system. Despite these limitations, ANN method outperforms the time series method in all time scale.

1.4.4. Hybrid Methods of Forecasting

The hybrid approach is a blend of various methodologies that are used to forecast precise wind speed and power over various time scales. The objective of the hybrid method is to get benefited from the merits of each method and obtain a worldwide best forecasting performance. Types of combinations are as follows:

- Combination of physical and statistical methods (time series)

- Combination of physical method along with statistical method (ANN)
- Combination of statistical method and novel method
- Combination of a novel method and a physical method
- Combination of statistical (time series) and statistical (ANN) method

Some of the hybrid methods are Evolutionary Computation (EC) + Fuzzy, Wavelet transform + Fuzzy, EC+ANN, Fuzzy + time series, ANN+NWP, NWP + time series, ANN + Fuzzy, and ANN + time series.

Hybrid methods advantages are that they avoids over training and high computation cost, achieve the optimal forecasting accuracy by reducing the forecasting error, avoids the local minima problem, and faster the convergence. Limitation of hybrid method is in some case, the single method outperforms the hybrid method.

1.5 Objectives of the Thesis

The aim of research is to improve the network from perturbation effects.

➢ To develop a model, that will provide improved weather prediction.

➢ To achieve higher accuracy using deep learning models.

➢ To do the short period weather condition based rapid prediction, using deep learning models.

➢ To evaluate our technique and compare it with several existing models for climate prediction.

1.6 Structural Organization of Thesis

We can find that weather forecasting has been an ever-challenging research area and if our prediction models keep in pace with the rapid changing environment we can minimize the loss of life and properties. Also, we can make the public well informed and updated with the natural calamities.

The thesis is divided into eight chapters. The contents of the thesis are organized as follows:

Chapter 1 contains the introduction that is the background, classification, and general methods of weather forecasting; it discusses the existing weather forecasting instruments and models. It also highlights the objectives and need for the research and its social significance.

Chapter 2 presents a broad literature review which includes the previous work related to the study. A thorough survey is done with importance given to papers, which narrates about implementation techniques and discusses about its experimental results along with its limitations.

Chapter 3 describes the general methodology used for forecasting with different models, which includes data collection, pre-processing of data, implementation setup, statistical and deep learning models used for training and different parametric evaluation metrics used for the evaluation process.

Chapter 4, 5 and 6 elaborates the construction and working of ARIMA, CRNN and proposed Hybrid_Stacked Bi-LSTM models respectively and how weather prediction model is designed using these models. For all the three models, their architecture is briefly presented and the results, screen shots and graphs are produced and elaborately discussed at the end of each model respectively.

Chapter 7 incorporates comparison and performance analysis of all three models on different parameters. It compares all the three methods adopted for weather forecasting, in terms of accuracy based on different error values that is MSE, RMSE, MAE and the results are validated. Appropriate charts and graphs are included to increase the quick interpretation of outputs.

Chapter 8 concludes this research works with the summary of the proposed models, major findings, its outcomes and limitations. The scope for further research is also discussed, which offers a great way to extend in different areas.

At last, list of references which are used for finalizing the work are cited.

CHAPTER-2

LITERATURE REVIEW

Chapter 2

Literature Review

There has been a wide range of research performed in the field related to weather forecasting to understand the ways of managing weather by using an appropriate form of forecasting since the technology started to evolve with time. This literature review is an evaluative report of facts and figures drawn from the literature in relation with the Weather Forecasting and Deep learning models. These reviews help in the description, summary, evaluation, substantiation, and clarification of the literature. This provides a theoretical foundation for the study and helps the authors in determining the study's scope. This review is a collection of academic papers that summarises the knowledge in the present scenario along with applicable findings and theoretical and methodological contributions in the field of weather forecasting.

The Literature review frames a background of the research and provides justification for carrying out the present research. It provided us with the clarity to learn from the preceding/ already existing theories about the Weather Forecasting. It demonstrated how the subject had previously been researched and highlighted errors and gaps in earlier studies.

Chapter two reviews the literature about Data Analytics; predictive analytics based deep learning models, previous work done on weather forecasting, usage of many machine learning and deep learning models for weather forecasting and challenges in weather forecasting. A thorough survey is done with importance given to papers, which narrates about the implementation techniques and discusses about its experimental results along with its limitations.

For the prediction of weather factors, meteorologists, scientists, and researchers have led to the development of numerous architectures, models, simulated systems, prototypes for attaining accuracy in forecast. Few literatures are summarized and highlighted below.

2.1 Introduction to Data Analytics

Data is defined as "factual information" in various forms like characters, numbers, images, audio and video which are used as bases for calculation, reasoning and discussion. Processing the data to enumerate assorted summaries and derived values to infer useful information is termed as data analysis. Dealing with the models, techniques, or methodologies to accomplish automated data analysis is defined as data analytics. Both these terms focus on the deed of goal but to differentiate them, data analytics can be interpreted as a subcomponent of data analysis that comprises the use of tools and techniques.

The sequence of data analysis based on its types and its functionality is shown in Figure as of three major types: Descriptive analytics, Predictive analytics and Prescriptive analytics [94]. From the Figure 2.1, it is clear that a general understanding of the data is very important before dealing with the data. Hence descriptive analytics is carried out first, next is predictive analytics and finally, prescribing a solution using prescriptive analytics is done.

Figure 2.1: Types of Data Analytics

Descriptive Analytics

Descriptive analytics is the anterior process of data analytics that aids in understanding the current state of the scenario and the reasoning behind the event that happened [95]. To carry out descriptive analytics, histories of data are examined and appropriate visualization techniques are used to find the facts [94]. Descriptive Analytics is also helpful in understanding the changes occurring in the data pattern over time and in figuring out the comparisons. Besides, it narrates the main features of the data such as mean, standard deviation, variance, quartiles, sum of squares, Root

Mean Square (RMS), frequency, etc., which are necessary for the subsequent stages of analytics.

Descriptive analytics is used to understand the circumstances using past and present data. Hence it acts as a base for predictive analytics by detecting the interval trends which are helpful to estimate future trends [96]. It uses statistical methods principally to summarize the knowledge patterns that comprise the following measures [97]

- Central Tendency Measures (Mean, Mode and Median)
- Dispersion/Variation Measures (Range, Variance and Standard Deviation)
- Position Measures (Percentile, Lower Quartile and Inter quartile)
- Frequency Measures (Ratio, Rate, Proportion and Percentage)

The above measures are simple. With the help of visualization techniques like probability distribution plot, box plot, scatter plot, histogram and bar chart, these measures will figure out the data patterns apparently.

Predictive Analytics

Predictive analytics assists in predicting or forecasting future possibilities and outcomes. It is essential to plan for the upcoming period [95]. This stage of analytics is necessary to take preventive measures if the outcomes predicted are detrimental to the intention. Prediction is a general term used to determine the unknown future outcomes whereas forecasting includes a temporal dimension to defend the subsequent outcomes. In the early days, predictive analytics was implemented using statistical method [94]. Currently, algorithms of Machine Learning (ML) and Artificial Neural Networks (ANN) play a predominant role in carrying out these analytics. Predictive modelling is mostly adopted in classification and clustering problems while the time series data utilizes the forecasting model.

Predictive analytics has gained more attention in the research community when compared to other types of analytics [96]. Probabilistic and progressive statistical methods like Bayesian, Markov Chain and Hidden Markov Chain are mostly used as prediction models [98]. These models help to estimate the likely occurrence of any event in the future and the knowledge inferred is represented through probability distribution [99]. Secondly, advanced statistical methods like regression, Auto Regressive Integrated Moving Average (ARIMA) and Support Vector Machine

(SVM) play a major role now in prediction and forecasting. In recent years, machine learning and data mining methods occupy a greater space in the domain of prediction.

Prescriptive Analytics

Prescriptive analytics is used to prescribe the finest course of action based on the predicted outcomes [100]. It also emphasizes the inference of recommended action thereby leading to optimal decision making which will help the society in many aspects. The inference from prediction may be a favourable or an unfavourable circumstance. Hence the community needs knowledge about the action to be taken to handle the situation. Thus, prescriptive analytics is considered as the esteemed level of analytics. The methodology used to implement prescriptive analytics is typically a blend of techniques such as mathematical programming, logic-based models etc., [99] which may also include predictive analytics occasionally.

Prescriptive analytics utilizes mathematical programming, logic-based models, evolutionary computation, simulation and sometimes probabilistic, machine learning methods also for better decision making. Mathematical programming includes linear and non-linear optimization, stochastic optimization, fuzzy linear optimization, and dynamic programming whereas evolutionary computations are comprised of algorithms like genetic, greedy and particle swarm optimization.

Data analytics can be of different types among which predictive and prescriptive analytics are considered to be important. However, prescriptive analytics proceeds after predictive analytics. Prediction problems are majorly categorized into classification and forecasting where classification deals with identifying the appropriate group for the given data and forecasting deals with generating future values based on the historical data. Forecasting includes the time component along with other exploratory variables used to predict future values whereas classification does not. Hence forecasting is applicable mostly for time series data which contains the attribute values on a constant interval of time such as hours, days, months, or years. As per the literature, ANN is efficient in handling non-linear data among other technique [101]. Hence it is preferred for both prediction and forecasting. RNN, which is a classification of ANN, is adopted to forecast the time series data since the previous state information is fed into the current state of RNN network. However, RNN suffers from certain issues like vanishing gradient due to back propagation and short-term memory. Hence complex units such as LSTM [102] are used in RNN for time series data.

Our work is for weather forecasting and for this predictive analysis plays a vital role. Hence further discussions and work will be done on the basis of predictive analytics.

2.2 Related Works on Predictive Analytics

Statistical methods were used predominantly before the emergence of ML methods and still, it's a challenging task to compete with statistical methods in terms of accuracy [103] but ML models, specifically ANNs are superior in certain aspects as follows:

- ANN can solve complex problems using non-linear functions whereas statistical methods can be solved using linear computation.
- ANN handles error reduction mechanism dynamically; however, this feature is not supported in statistical methods.
- ANN focuses more on accuracy whereas statistical methods express more on the relationship between the variables.
- ANN does not expect a correlation between the variables, but statistical methods perform prediction based on it.
- Impact of missing values and outliers is less in prediction for ANNs where as statistical methods have more impact.

RNN for Time Series Data:

In 1950s, Markov chain and Hidden Markov models (HMM) were used for the time series forecast. However, there was an exponential growth of state space. Present state prediction is dependent only upon the immediate former state. Due to these reasons, those models are impractical in the computation of long-range dependencies [104]. When RNN emerged in 1986 [105], it comprised of network memory formed due to the recurrent connections. This feature allowed the hidden units to view their previous outputs. Then it was modified later to interact with the previous states within the internal network. It leaves the predicted outcome to the outside world [106]. With the above-mentioned functionalities, RNN learns to forecast for more time lags than previous models [107]. Back propagation persists a chief role in reducing the error and loss of the network. It brings the predicted value closer to the actual value thereby

21

improving the accuracy level during the training phase of ANNs. This is achieved by propagating the error back to the nodes through the chain rule of partial derivatives of the activation function for weight adjustment in the network.

Unlike other ANNs, unfolded network like RNN handles back propagation differently. It calculates ordered derivative [108] to train the network across several time steps using back propagation. This is termed as Back propagation through Time (BPTT). Thus, BPTT makes RNN a powerful network with memory to store multiple periods. But neural networks with basic back propagation do not have memory since they rely only on the previous one-time step.

Even though RNN is superior in several ways compared to conventional ANNs, it finds difficulty in learning the long-range dependencies. The following are the major reasons:

- Vanishing gradient problem after certain time steps during back propagation
- Network becoming unstable due to exploding gradient problem
- Limited storage capability

Vanishing Gradient Problem

There are many solutions contributed by the researchers to the vanishing gradient problem to improvise the learning on long-term dependencies. Vanishing gradient problem occurs as a result of error signal flow back in time over a recurrent network where the gradient decreases exponentially on training the network using gradient descent methods. When the error backflow vanishes, there is no effect on weight updates in the network. Hence a gradient must exist to obtain appropriate weight for better accuracy with minimum error.

As a first try, researchers tried utilizing global search methods like simulated annealing, random weight guessing along with multi-grid random search, which do not use gradient information. But they do not work well with networks having a larger number of parameters, taking more training time and being devoid of precise computation [109]. As a next try, time weighted Pseudo-Newton algorithm introduced a constant _ to forbid large variation in weight. However, it encountered the worst performance on increasing the sequence length [110].

Then discrete error propagation was adopted to enforce the gradients by propagating discrete error information through the units that compute non-differential function called hard threshold. This method performs faster, is robust to local minima and handles increasing sequence length compared to global search methods. Even though discrete error propagation avoids the gradients to vanish, it fails in successful learning of real-valued information over time and the algorithm undertakes local random search which produces an irregular learning curve [109].

It was stated that gradient decay is also necessary to store discrete state information for long-term but exponential decay in long-term gradients tends to make the short-term gradients influence completely since the total gradient is the sum of both [111]. Another BPTT method was introduced namely Truncated BPTT (TBPTT) that propagates back to a few steps instead of entire time steps which reduces the computation along with adequate approximation to the true gradient [112].

Like TBPTT, epoch wise BPTT trains the network over a single epoch with a longer time step than TBPTT, but both are effective online algorithms; they cannot be used for offline datasets. Generally, BPTT methods cannot account for noise in the process. However, they are relatively quick and exact, so it is preferable to use them in RNN. The idea of increasing the learning rate and the number of units within the network does not make impact and hence no increase in the error flow noted since BPTT is sensitive to recent distractions.

Exploding Gradient Problem

Sometimes there is a sudden increase in error. This blows up the error gradient which makes the network unstable without converging to the learning process. This is called exploding gradient problem, even when the learning rate is very small in RNN [113]. The error curves will have several steep jumps with no stable limit cycle in the neighbourhood which leads to numerical overflow during the exploding gradient. Hence the network has to start the learning again. This spike of time is called bifurcation point.

To handle the above-mentioned situation, "teacher forcing" technique is used with multiple attractor points to avoid saddle-node bifurcations. Teacher forcing method uses the tactic of replacing the actual output rather than the desired output for the subsequent computations of RNN [114] which results in stable learning. This method was proven in it reducing the exploding gradient and working in unbounded memory

23

too. The downside was to assign the target at every time step which may not be known in prior always, asymptotic behaviour too.

Truncated BPTT was a good solution for the exploding gradient problem since the error is propagated back to a few time steps only as specified in the previous subsection. Therefore, it avoids the instability in learning equations. Fixing the legitimate number of time steps to back propagate is a challenging task in TBPTT since the same value cannot be taken up for any input sequence length.

Limited Storage Capability

RNN is superior in dealing with time series data for the reason of retaining memory which is not obtainable in feed forward networks. The recurrent connections of RNN yield the network with memory to employ previous output to the current state in the hidden unit. The hidden units of RNN are capable of providing infinite memory on the occasion that the activation function is analog, but memory is always bounded for the sake of limited numeric precision in the machines [106]. Network memory gets decayed exponentially in RNN on repetitive execution of activation function to store the changes in weight, relevant parameters, and internal preceding states. Thus, it is unable to exploit the full capacity of the network.

Because of the difficulties faced as mentioned above, a finite-state learning system called "state network" was developed which persists in one among n discrete states at a time t and it back propagates to a discrete distribution of targets. Additional optimization criteria were needed for this method whenever target information was not diffused over all the states during back propagation.

Formulation of LSTM

To address the obstacles faced by RNN as explained in the previous subsections, a distinct architecture called Long Short-Term Memory was proposed in 1997 [115]. General RNN is extended with special gates in the internal units to form LSTM and it retains constant error flow in it. LSTM contains two multiplicative units as quoted below to defend error flow from unwanted perturbations,

- Input gate unit to protect the memory content of the current unit from irrelevant inputs.

24

- Output gate unit to protect the network memory of other units from irrelevant contents stored in the current unit.

Incorporating the input and output gate in the hidden unit of RNN results in the complex architecture called memory cell. The memory cell is erected with a central linear unit with fixed self-connection called Constant Error Carrousel (CEC) which is the central feature of LSTM to avoid vanishing gradient problems and to bridge longer time lags. The input and output activation of the current internal unit is accomplished by sigmoid function with random weights assigned and tanh function to update the current memory cell. During forward propagation, the input gate decides whether to override the information in the memory cell or to retain the same content and the output gate decides the access of memory cell by the current unit along with preventing other units from being perturbed.

CEC plays a major role in back propagation by setting up the weight of self-connected recurrent edge as one that enforces constant error flow to be propagated. This makes the activation remain constant and the function as linear in the current unit. The gate units are responsible to release/allow the error from/to CEC with appropriate scaling. The parameter values of multiplicative gate units and CEC are not accumulated out of the current internal state. So the model was defined as truncated LSTM with the following advantages,

- Constant error back propagation within the memory cell facilitates the network to handle long time lags.
- It can handle the noise and continuous values.
- It supports an unlimited number of states without the necessity of defining it prior.
- Learns quickly to distinguish disparate occurrences in the input sequence.
- Fine tuning the parameters is not required.
- It is local in both time as well as space hence both the complexities are $O(W)$ where W is known to be the number of weights.

LSTM contributes a solution for certain issues faced by conventional RNN especially vanishing gradient problem, performs prediction for longer input sequence and utilizes memory of the network in an efficient manner. However, the memory is to be reset for every input sequence to handle long-term dependencies which becomes the reason for adding the forget gate in it. LSTM does not explicitly discuss the solution for the exploding gradient problem also.

LSTM With Forget Gate

Over several highlights of LSTM, there was a challenge in handling continual time series because the cell state of the network may grow linearly in an unlimited fashion for continuous input streams. This causes the output squashing function to saturate thereby forging its derivative to vanish. Hence incoming errors are blocked during back propagation. This situation was handled wisely by replacing CEC of standard LSTM with an adaptive "forget gate" in 1999 which learns to reset itself at appropriate times [116].To activate the forget gate, the sigmoid function is used. The forget gate was initialized to positive values which means its activation was almost 1.0 at the initial stages of the training phase that behaves as standard LSTM.

Once the forget gate learns to identify the useless memory contents, its activation becomes zero and the memory blocks the out-of-date contents which are reset thereby affording space for further input sequences. The core idea behind the forget gate is to allow the storage until it gets trained to grasp the variation between relevant and irrelevant information. Later it preserves the internal state from irrelevant content by flushing them out. This extended LSTM with forget gate is also local in space and time as standard LSTM and the space complexity does not depend on input sequence length. The problem of limited storage capability of RNN is solved to a significant level by LSTM with forget gate and this model is used widely compared to the other versions of LSTM.

LSTM is a well-suited framework for time series prediction with an acceptable level of performance. Most of the LSTM models are adopted for the applications like speech recognition, handwriting recognition and NLP. Also, the majority of these applications are classification-based prediction and analysis. Research works related to forecasting are fewer especially in the field of hydrology. The importance of rainfall prediction is explored in the introduction chapter and the following section discloses the survey related to rainfall forecasting using several ML methods. Finally, the issues in the existing models are explained thereby proving that LSTM is advisable for rainfall prediction with a novel approach.

2.3 Work Related to Weather Forecasting

For the scientific community, accurate weather forecasting is a big challenge. Computer models, observation, and knowledge of weather trends and patterns are all used in weather prediction modelling. Forecasts can be made using the methods mentioned above that are reasonably accurate.

Several research have been done or being done for weather forecasting. Accurate, fast, and reliable weather forecasting poses a major challenge to the scientific community. A rainfall prediction model involves synchronization of various numerical computer models, observations from different sources and knowledge of past and current weather trends and patterns. By the use of these methods along with the expertise of forecaster's knowledge, accuracy in the forecasts can be attained.

Shared Nearest Neighbor (SNN) clustering by Michael Steinbach et al.[117] has shown to find such kind of homogeneous clusters. Out of it each cluster has a centroid, which is the average of all the time series representing the ocean locations in the cluster, and hence these centroids can be used to identify prospective climate indicators.

The authors used a technique of sequential pattern mining as explained by Han and Kamber [118] in 2001. The concluding remarks by the authors are interesting and are quoted below; "Given the small number of simulations, the results reported in the paper are only the beginning of what will a very exciting collaboration between meteorology and computer sciences…" During the same period, Pabreja [119] had presented the concept paper during an international conference at Indian national centre for medium range forecasting (NCMRWF) where a large number of international meteorologists were present. The concept according to the meteorological community was novel and need trial.

Godfrey C. Onwubolu et al. [120], in 2007 has presented the use of data mining activities, in weather forecasting. In, the self-organizing data mining approach, they have implemented enhanced Group Method of Data Handling (e-GMDH). The weather data includes temperature and pressure on daily basis along with monthly rainfall. Concluded with a good accuracy and warns against using unnormalized data points or outliers, as could lead to give unrealistic results which may affect our knowledge inference, in weather forecasting.

27

Cadenas et al.[121], in 2007 have proposed the ARIMA and the ANN models for wind speed forecasting based on seven years of recorded wind speed data. The performance of the proposed model was evaluated using MSE, MAE, and MAPE. The output results show the seasonal ARIMA providing good accuracy for the prediction of wind speed. However, the performance required improvement by increasing the number of training values for the ANN model.

Bilgili et al.[122], in 2007 have utilized the Resilient Propagation neural network system for the prediction of speed of the wind. The prediction of the speed of wind of any station is dependent upon the data of the wind speed of its nearby stations which are designated as the reference stations. The obtained predicted values by the ANN were compared with the actual value, and that the maximum mean absolute error was found as 14.13% while the minimum was 4.49%.

Lopez et al.[123], in 2008 have introduced an ANN method for effective access to the annual average wind speed at a particular site. They used a Bayesian regularization algorithm to train the Multilayer perceptron network with 15 neurons hidden layer. The number of input parameters needed for neural network architecture was analyzed, and it recommends that wind speed and wind direction data are essential. In an intricate landscape area, wind direction will be an important input parameter that can decrease Root Mean Square (RMS) by 23%. The result exhibited the ANN method can be used as a consistent estimate of wind speeds at a designated location.

Meteorological environment of a tornado outbreak in Southern Romania has been studied by Oprea and Bell [124], in 2009. Three tornadoes were reported in Southern Romania on May 2005 that caused severe damage. The synoptic and mesoscale conditions associated with these tornadoes were analyzed using ECMWF and ALADIN model outputs. The analysis results of ECMWF model confirmed that the vertical profile of the wind showed a veering of the wind at low levels. Also, the vertical profiles of the wind depicted strong vertical shear at low and mid-levels.

Li and Shi [125], in 2010 presented the utilization of different neural network systems in the forecasting of wind speed. The wind speed data observed from two places in North Dakota was used for training and testing the networks. There are three kinds of characteristics that ANN includes an adaptive linear element, back propagation, and radial basis function was investigated. The accuracy of the output achieved by these three ANN models was evaluated in terms of MAE, MAPE and RMSE. The least prediction MAPE achieved for a radial base function network was

28

0.189%. Thus, the results indicated the absence of outperformance from ANN model for the same wind speed data. Furthermore, the selection of which kind of ANNs for good results was mainly reliant on the data input.

Juraj Bartoka et al.[126], in 2010, in their paper came out with meteorological detection and prediction of weather factors based on synoptic, statistical and climatological models integrated with the knowledge discovery process.

Liu et al.[127], in 2012 have used a hybrid model for prediction of wind speed. The EMD method was applied, and then the original datasets were converted into multiple numbers of different sub-series. Afterward, ANN was used for building a predictive model and made the multi-step prediction on each sub-series. Finally, all the prediction results were combined in the sub-series to achieve the final prediction of wind speed. The hybrid model performance was related to an ANN model and an ARIMA model. The wind speed results indicated the accuracy of the hybrid model as acceptable and useful in handling the non-stationary time series data.

Liu et al.[128], in 2012 have proposed a hybrid model derived from ARIMA-ANN and ARIMA-Kalman procedures for prediction of the speed of wind. An ANN model for a segment of the wind speed sample was created. During this modeling process, a time series ARIMA was utilized to choose its best structure. A Kalman model was built for the same segment of the wind speed data. A time series ARIMA was utilized for obtaining the best parameters of the Kalman model. The author's proposed two hybrid methods and their accuracy were evaluated. Both models demonstrated good performance, which could be used for the wind speed prediction.

Kumar Abhishek et al.[129], in 2012 used ANN for forecasting the maximum temperature for a whole year with varying transfer functions, hidden layers and neurons to handle over fitting with the aim to increase efficiency in prediction.

Ulf Johansson et al.[130], in 2013 proposed a new model for predictive framework for conformal prediction using classification method, namely decision trees. Their experimental results justified that decision tree is efficient and can be combined with many decision trees for maximum accuracy.

Akashdeep Gupta et al. [131], in 2013 used Time series analysis for forecasting Indian rainfall. Their conclusion is that as the hidden neurons increases, the error is decreased to a certain limit and after that it begins to increase due to the noise in the network. Larger number of hidden neurons in the network is representative of greater nonlinearity in the data.

Mahmudur Rahman et al. [132], in 2013 compared ANFIS with ARIMA on the data between 2000 to 2009 based on Maximum Temperature, Minimum Temperature, Humidity and Air Pressure on various performance metrics and found that ARIMA gives better result than ANFIS.

Piyush Kapoor and Sarabjeet Singh Bedi, in 2013 [133] used sliding window Algorithm for weather forecasting and states that the method is quite efficient for weather prediction with an average accuracy rate of 92.2 %.

Pinky Saikia Dutta and Hitesh Tahbilder [134], in 2014 exploited data mining techniques for prediction of rainfall in Assam. This was carried out using traditional statistical technique -Multiple Linear Regression. R-squared parameter is used to measure the performance of this model. Experimental results show that the prediction model based on multiple linear regressions produces acceptable accuracy.

An early paper of this domain by B. Ustaoglu [135], tests three different kind of ANN based methods: (1) feed-forward back propagation (FFBP), (2) radial basis function (RBF) and, (3) generalized regression neural network (GRNN). It compares the answers with traditionally used multiple linear regression (MLR), they obtained notable improvements over MLR outputs. A paper written in 2015 by Z. Karevan [136] described a black box idea: use of Machine learning methods such as k-NN and Elastic Net for the process of feature selection then trains model using Support Vector Machine Regression with Least Square loss function to predict minimum and maximum temperature. After 3 years, R. Isabelle used Recurrent Convolutional Neural Networks for weather forecasting and visualization [137] where they propose use of convolution filters + LSTMs. Their results were found substantially better in comparison with popular methods.

Another approach was used by P. Hewage [138], where they used multiple features like temperature, pressure, wind, humidity, precipitation and moisture to predict future value of the same feature. This was executed by implementing several machine learning and deep learning algorithms like TCN [139], LSTM with multi-input multi-output(MIMO) and multi-input single-output(MISO) methods. S. Kendzierski used a novel approach by implementing Jordan Pi-Sigma Neural Network (JPSN) for time series data, introduced by N. Husaini[140]. In this paper they combined two methodologies: Jordan Neural Network, Pi-Sigma Neural Network to predict the temperature. The MSE of the model is remarkably low, but model does not satisfy the criteria suggested by A. Kumar [141] and the performance of the model can be acceptable if: NMSE ≤ 0.5.

Mustafa Gockenet al.[142], in 2015 adopted three different techniques, namely, ANN (Artificial Neural Network), ANFIS (Adaptive Network Based Fuzzy Inference System), and MRA (Multiple Regression Analysis) for weather forecasting. They have designed the model to forecast daily average temperature. To judge the forecasting the performance measures they had used statistical indicators, namely Mean Absolute Percent Error (MAPE), Mean Square Error (MSE), Mean Absolute Deviation (MAD), Root-Mean Squared Error (RMSE), etc. The results were compared and found that ANFIS exhibited best forecasting performance than ANN and MRA.

Another hybrid ARIMA-ANN model with increased predicting accuracy was presented by Khashei et al. [143]. The ARIMA model is fitted directly to the given time series in their model, and a single data value is anticipated. The time series, ARIMA forecast value, and forecast error are then sent into ANN, which calculates future values. This model outperformed the preceding ARIMA and ANN models in terms of forecast accuracy.

In 2015, Moinul Hossain et al. [144] compared two approaches used for the prediction of temperature of air from historical pressure, humidity, and temperature data collected from the meteorological sensors in Northwestern Nevada, finding that a DNN with Stacked Denoising Auto-Encoders (SDAE) performs much better than a standard multilayer feed forward network for prediction.

In 2015, Afan Galih Salman et al.[145] examined the prediction performance of RNN, Conditional Restricted Boltzmann Machine (CRBM), and CN models. The BMKG (Indonesian Agency for Meteorology, Climatology, and Geophysics) data set, which was collected from 1973 to 2009 with various weather stations in the Aceh area, and the EI-Nino Southern Oscilation (ENSO) data set, which was provided by international institutions such as the National Weather Service Center for Environmental Prediction Climate Change (NOAA). The findings of this study are likely to help with weather forecasting in a variety of applications.

A weather forecasting model was presented by Aditya Grover et al.[146], in 2015 considered joint influence of key variables of weather to make predictions. Also, a data-centric kernel was introduced and showed with the use of GPR, can effectively interpolate over space by taking turbulence into account. An improved system with a deep belief network and tuned parameters comes in existence to model the dependencies amongst various weather variables. Experiments incorporated with real-world data shows better outcomes with the new methodology than NOAA benchmarks

Wang et al. [147] assumed the time series data to be a multiplication of a nonlinear and a linear series, in contrast to additive hybrid models. The ARIMA model is fitted to the given time series data and an ARIMA forecast is calculated in their hybrid model. After that, removing ARIMA projections from the original series yields the residual error series. To get forecasts, the obtained residual error series is considered as nonlinear and modelled using ANN. ARIMA forecasts are multiplied by ANN forecasts to get the final forecasts. In three-time series, this model showed better performance than the other models in terms of forecast accuracy. The approach, however, cannot be used on a series where ARIMA predictions contain zero.

Inspired by Babu et al. [148], Oliveira et al. [149] used an exponential smoothing filter to divide the time series data into low-volatile and high-volatile series, and then further divided the high-volatile series into linear and nonlinear series.

The low-volatile series, linear series and nonlinear series are handled using ARIMA model, AR (p) model and support vector regression (SVR) model respectively. In addition, the model parameters are optimized using particle swarm optimization (PSO). This hybrid model provided better forecasting accuracy than Babu et al. [148] model considering 13 time series datasets. However, these models loose data points while decomposing the time series using moving average or exponential smoothing filter. Therefore, these models are not appropriate for smaller time series because less data will remain to build the model. One may develop a decomposition method without losing data, so that the hybrid method based on data decomposition techniques can be suitably applied on smaller time series also.

A deep neural network architecture was presented by Mohamed Akram Zaytarand Chaker El Amrani, in 2016 [150] for time series weather prediction. Multi stacked LSTMs were used to map sequences of weather values for short term forecast of Temperature, Humidity and Wind Speed data. To train the model, hourly meteorological data of 15 years from 2000 to 2015 was used and results show that proposed model was competitive and considered to be better alternative when compared to traditional methods for the forecasting of general weather conditions.

A trial was done by P. Srikanth et al. [151], in 2016 for the estimation of the missing data by using three methods i.e. ANFIS, ARIMA and polynomial curve fitting for the forecasting of weather and analyzed that polynomial curve fitting based on fuzzy logic works better on various performance parameters like SSE, RMSE, MAE and R^2.

T.R.V. Anandharajanet al.[152], in 2016 used machine learning based intelligent prediction. Linear regression was used for the analysis and prediction of next day's weather with good accuracy of more than 90%, on the basis of the dataset.

Mark Holmstrom et al. [153], in 2016 used machine learning for the long term weather predictions. Two models were used; first one was linear regression model and second was a functional regression model with variation. Professional weather forecasting services outperformed both the models for short term, while for longer span of time these models outperformed professional ones. Similarly in 2018 Sue Ellen Haupt et al. [154] used machine learning for applied weather prediction and as a result The Dynamic Integrated forecasting System was evolved which was one of the first automated weather forecasting engines.

Amir Ghaderi et al.[155], in 2017 used deep learning along with RNN to forecast the wind speed with improvised short term results compared to other models. The time series data was taken from the windmills of northeast US for the research and proved to be improvised in terms of forecasting.

Gaurav Chavan and Dr. Bashirahamad Momin [156], in 2017 worked on Structural and weather forecasting algorithms based on Time Series like Linear Regression, MLR, SVR and ARIMA. The RMSE parameter was used for computation to measure the predictive ability, which indicates ARIMA as the best prediction model.

Diksha Khiatani and Dr. Udayan Ghose [157], in 2017 worked on Hidden Markov Model for weather prediction. In the work HMM was used for the prediction using Markov Chain property. For calculations, Weather data of last twenty-one years was observed for the training of the model along with the probability of occurrence of an event. The result shows the reliability of model for the prediction of following five days' weather depending upon the today's weather pattern.

In 2017, Karthika. S. et al. [158] worked on short-term load forecasting to measure meteorological conditions and anticipate hourly demand using a hybrid model, ARIMA – SVM. ARIMA is utilised to anticipate demand after correcting outliers using Percentage Error (PE), and SVM is used for deviation correction, resulting in a lower MAPE error and faster convergence.

SanamNarejo and Eros Pasero in 2017 [159] applied deep learning approach for weather parameters predictions like temperature, pressure and humidity of a particular location and results shows a high degree of accuracy with this feature based forecasting model in the predictions also implies that for long term forecasting this model can suitably adopted over huge geographic locations.

Rashmi Bhardwaj and Varsha Duhoon [160], in 2018 published a paper on Weather Forecasting using Soft Computing and Statistical Techniques. They had combined both Adaptive Neuro-Fuzzy Inference System (ANFIS) and multiple linear regression (MLR) models to analyze meteorological data sets. The performance of the two models was compared using root mean square error (RMSE), and it was discovered that the ANFIS model outperformed the multiple linear regression (MLR) models with reduced prediction error.

Afan Galih Salman et al. in 2018 [161] used LSTM model variant for the prediction of ground visibility and analyzed that predicting capabilities of the model can be improvised with the use of moderating variables. Based on experimental outcomes, improved accuracy obtained with the proposed merged-LSTM model by 4.8% higher.

Dires Negash Fente and Prof. Dheeraj Kumar Singh in 2018 [162] worked on RNN with LSTM for weather prediction. Various weather parameters were collected from NCDC and for different combinations of weather parameters neural network was trained after using LSTM technique. For predicting the future weather condition by the use of LSTM, the neural network is trained by the use of various combinations of weather parameters i.e. temperature, precipitation, wind speed, pressure and humidity. Prediction accuracy obtained with this method was found to be better than existing methods.

In 2019 a data-driven extreme framework for weather prediction based on deep learning pattern-recognition methods and analog forecasting was proposed by Ashesh Chattopadhyay et al. [163] and the results showed the accuracy and extremely faster weather forecasts.

In 2019, Yuhu Zhang et al. [164] examined the drought predicting abilities of ARIMA, WNN, and SVM in the Sanjiang Plain, China. The models employed in this study were based upon the standard precipitation evapotranspiration index (SPEI) on a 12-month timeline, which was calculated by the use of data collected from seven meteorological sites between 1979 and 2016. After that, the prediction of SPEI series was done with the ARIMA, WNN and SVM models separately. To evaluate the performance, various parametric measure like R^2 (The coefficient of determination), MSE (mean-squared error), NSE (Nash–Sutcliffe efficiency) along with nonparametric measure like Kolmogorov–Smirnov (K–S) distance were used and the results shows that ARIMA model performs better than WNN and SVM models.

Siamak Mehrkanoon in 2019 [165] introduces new deep convolutional neural networks (CNN) based data-driven predictive models for the prediction of temperature and wind speed. On comparison with the classical neural networks utilized for modeling nonlinear systems, the proposed models give excellent results in the form of improved prediction performance.

Bin Wang et al. in 2019 [166] introduced a new machine learning based method for weather forecasting i.e. deep uncertainty quantification (DUQ). The prediction model was trained using a newly formulated loss function known as negative log-likelihood error (NLE), that is proficient of inferring sequential point estimation and prediction interval at the same time. The results show that NLE loss training improves point estimation generalization significantly.

Nitin Singh et al. in 2019 [167] proposed a machine learning based low cost, reliable, and efficient application for weather forecasting by using Python on Raspberry Pi board and as a result accuracy score of 87.90% was obtained with this model.

Pradeep Hewage et al. in 2020 [138] proposed a short term, Deep learning based weather forecasting data-driven model by using temporal modeling approaches of LSTM along with temporal convolutional networks (TCN) and its performance was compared with the existing ML approaches, a dynamic ensemble method and statistical forecasting approaches, also with weather research and forecasting (WRF) NWP model and results shows increased efficiency up to 12 hours.

Afan Galih Salmana and Bayu Kanigoro in 2020 [168] used ARIMA model for visibility forecasting for the variant values of p,d,q parameters and the work gives better results in terms of MSE.

Rafaela Castro et al. in 2020 [169] proposed a deep learning architecture STConvS2S (Spatiotemporal Convolutional Sequence to Sequence Network), for the purpose of learning spatial as well as temporal data dependencies using only convolutional layers. Two limitations of convolutional networks were resolved to predict sequences using past data i.e. (i) During the learning process, the temporal order is violated and

35

(ii) The Length of input and output sequences are required to be equal. Computational experiments show that results obtained with it outperforms or matches the results of state-of-the-art architectures in forecasting.

In 2020, Zao Zhang and Yuan Dong [170] used neural network and future temperature is predicted using past temperature values. Specifically, a convolutional recurrent neural network (CRNN) model based on CNN and RNN was developed, which uses neural networks to learn the time and space correlation of temperature changes from historical data. Daily temperature data from mainland China was used as training data for the model, and the results reveal a temperature forecast with an error of roughly 0.907°C.

Zarif Al Sadeque and Francis M. Bui [171] used a deep learning approach to Predict weather data using cascaded LSTM network in 2020, which uses the LSTM layers with a varied number of units in each layer in a stacked fashion. For a given time sequence, multiple weather variables were taken as input features to forecast the similar weather parameters in a multi-input multi-output (MIMO) structure. Testing was done on resulting models to predict the wind speed, humidity and temperature and experimented with variety of hyper-parameters consisting a number of LSTM layers, a variable learning rate, number of LSTM units and the outcome shows that for the shorter period prediction, the cascaded models performs better than the state of art LSTM or 1D CNN.

In a survey done by K.U. Jaseena and Binsu C. Kovoor [172] on intelligent predictors based Deterministic weather forecasting models in 2020 and discussed recent weather forecasting related work and analyzed the results. In the evaluation of the existing methods Identified limitation was lack of stability assessment. They have also concluded that reliability of ANN and SVM is greater for weather forecasting amongst machine learning techniques. Deep learning architectures with neural networks and hybrid models are offering excellent results in present scenario.

Debneil Saha Roy, in 2020 [173] worked on the forecasting of air temperature using deep neural networks over two forecast horizons and uses MLP, LSTM and a combination of LSTM and CNN. The outcome of the work shows that the combination of LSTM and CNN works much better than the other models and at both the forecast horizons it outperforms other models. And also in a review done by Jenny Cifuentes et al. [174] deep learning models performs better than ANN for air temperature prediction in terms of mean square error

Trang Thi Kieu Tranet et al. in 2020 [175] worked on deep learning based forecasting of maximum temperature. The deep learning network structure was optimized with the use of meta-learning principles for hyper parameter optimization. To select the optimal network architecture, genetic algorithm (GA) for meta-learning was used and three different models ANN, RNN and LSTM were tested and trained with the use of similar dataset and outcome of the work shows that for long time forecasting the hybrid model of an LSTM network with GA gives better results than other models. Also, James N.K. Liu et al.[176] states that a better feature space is provided by Deep neural network for weather data sets to predict the change in weather for coming 24 hours.

Kartika Purwandari et al. in 2020 [177] used application of machine learning on Twitter data about the weather and used three methods (SVM, MNB, and LR) for the work, the SVM was proved to be superior amongst these with 93% accuracy.

A H M Jakaria et al. in 2020 [178] did a case study on weather forecasting using machine learning .In this work, a technology based on machine learning (ML) was presented for weather forecasting and evaluation results show that accurate weather features can be predicted by machine learning models and proved to be better than traditional approaches.

A research article of Stephan Rasp et al. was published in 2020 [179] based on a benchmark data set for data-driven weather forecasting, focused on medium range prediction with the hope of improvisation in the results in data driven approach of weather forecasting.

"Deep learning-based weather prediction (DLWP) is expected to be a strong method and outperform almost all the conventional methods". In a survey performed on Deep Learning-Based Weather Prediction (DLWP) done by Xiaoli Ren et al. in 2020 [180], the state-of-art studies for weather forecasting based on deep learning, in the aspects of the design of neural network (NN) architectures, spatial and temporal scales was done and analyzed the pros and cons of DLWP by comparing it with the conventional NWP.

Anatoliy Doroshenko et al. in 2020 [181] proposed a neural network architecture for the correction in the regional numerical model errors and to improvise 2m temperature forecasting. The proposed work improves the 2m temperature forecasting in approximately 50% cases.

In 2021, Steven Dewitteet al.[48] compared numerical weather prediction model with deep learning model and found that in terms of computing power, Traditional NWP models are challenging and for probabilistic forecasting it needs to run several times whereas Deep Learning models need a high computing power only for the duration of offline training phase and they can be very efficient for online execution. Also M. G. Schultz et al. [182] in the same year, concludes that there is a possibility that Deep learning approaches may replace the current numerical weather models and data assimilation systems.

In the work done by Matthew Chantry et al. in 2021 [183] for operational weather forecasting systems, machine learning was accessed as an accelerator for the parameterization schemes and it was found that the emulator on which work was in progress was found to be more accurate for medium range forecasting than the version of the parameterization scheme, used for operational predictions.

Selim Furkan Tekin et al. in 2021 [184] worked on a model for weather forecasting, composed of Convolutional LSTM, and CNN units with encoder-decoder structure. Short as well as long term performance and interpretability was enhanced with a context matcher mechanism. With this model, excellent validation and test score was scored amongst most of the baseline models, including ConvLSTM forecasting network and U-Net.

Tingzhao Yu et al. in 2021 [185] proposed a novel approach for meteorological forecasting. To find out more discriminative spatial–temporal features, a cascaded module was introduced which was simple but effective. One more memory module (Axial attention) was proposed to get long-term spatial–temporal dependence. Both the modules were combined with standard ConvGRU resulting in ATMConvGRU, hence producing improvised future predictions when experimented on current weather details.

SachinSoni et al. in 2021 [186] worked on weather prediction based on a window algorithm slide. The outcomes suggest that the utilization of the method was effective for weather forecasting with an average accuracy of 94.2%.

Ayman M. Abdalla et al. conducted a research survey on several deep learning weather prediction (DLWP) methodologies utilised to construct data-driven weather forecasting systems in 2021 [187]. When compared to the widely used Numerical Weather Prediction, DL applications have shown to be quite promising in terms of results (NWP).

Table 2.1 shows a summary of the state of-the-art weather forecasting models which can be used in the forecasting of weather with their merits and demerits.

Table 2.1 Comparison of various state of-the-art weather forecasting models.

Weather Forecasting Model	Merits	Demerits
Computer algorithms based early weather forecasting models (Innocenti et al., 2017 [188]; Reddy and Babu, 2017) [189].	Uses computer devices for calculations. Hydrostatic. Ideal for limited area forecasting. Available the open-source code. Ideal for area-specific weather forecasting with a limited number of parameters.	Uses complex statistical-based and non-linear mathematical equations. High use of computer power. Need a detailed understanding of algorithms. Requires long processing time. Requires constant adjustment to manage a perfect weather forecast.
WRF model (Powers et al., 2017 [190]; Skamarock et al., 2008) [191].	Uses computer devices to calculations. Enables vertical coordination to track atmospheric pressure. Open source. Ability to establish two-way communication through nesting. Provide effective weather forecasting at the global level or regional level.	Uses complex non-linear mathematical equations. Requires high computation. As the time difference between now and the forecast time grows, the forecast becomes less reliable. It is necessary to attain a better understanding of the model, its implementation along with the various solutions available.
Global Spectral Model (Díaz et al., 2016 [192]; Tenzer, 2017) [193]	Uses computer devices to calculations. High-resolution medium-range weather forecasting. Open-source.	Uses complex non-linear mathematical equations. Requires high computation. Needs a greater understanding of the model. Requires long processing time.
UM (Unified Model) (Cullen, 1993[194]; Kelly et al., 2019) [195].	Uses computer devices for calculations. Non-hydrostatic. Two-way communication through nesting. Can use for both global and regional level. Not requires a detailed understanding of algorithms	Requires high computation for solving complex non-linear mathematical equations. Requires long processing time. Less reliable when the difference between the current time and the forecast time is increased. Needs a greater understanding of the model for installation.

Weather Forecasting Model	Merits	Demerits
Aviation Model (AVN) (Xue et al., 2003)[196].	Uses computer devices. Hydrostatic. High accuracy for a limited number of parameters, such as wind, turbulence. Open source. Update regularly.	Limited information about the weather about aviation-related factors. Uses complex non-linear mathematical equations and high computer power. Requires long processing time and understanding of the model.
High Resolution Limited Area Model (HIRLAM) (Cats and Wolters, 1996 [197]; Korsholm et al., 2008) [198].	Uses computer devices. Regional weather forecast. Open source.	Large systems of mathematical equations and requires high computer power. Not suitable for large-area forecasting. Requires long processing time. An essential requirement to a detailed understanding of the model.
Regional Atmospheric Modelling System (RAMS) (Cotton et al., 2003 [199]; Gómez et al., 2016) [200].	Calculations are carried through high-performance computer devices. Non hydrostatic. Can use for both global and regional level. Not requires a detailed understanding of algorithms	Solving mathematical problems necessitates a lot of computing power. It takes a long time to process. This is not an open source model. As the difference between now and the anticipated time grows, the forecast becomes less reliable.
European Centre for Medium-Range Weather Forecasts (ECMWF) (Benedetti et al., 2009[201]; Rémy et al., 2019) [202].	Ideal for global weather forecasting. Can be used for regional forecasting. Uses computers to solve complex mathematical equations. Non hydrostatic. It is not essential to have a detailed understanding of algorithms.	For regional forecasting, there is less resolution. To solve nonlinear mathematical equations, enormous computer power is required. This is not an open source model. As the time difference between now and the anticipated time grows, the forecast becomes less reliable.

According to Section 2.3 and Table 2.1, there are several challenges identified in the NWP models. The common challenges are that they use high computing power to execute many non-linear simultaneous equations, and it requires a long time for processing. Besides, most of the models discussed in Table 2.1 are suitable for global or regional weather forecasting. As stated in Section 2.3, the data-driven computer modelling systems can be utilized for the reduction of the computational power of NWP systems [203].

Specifically, ML and deep learning are capable of capturing the nonlinear or complex underlying characteristics of a physical process along with the higher degree of accuracy[204].

2.4 Machine learning and Deep learning

2.4.1 Machine Learning

Machine Learning (ML) is a prominent subject of discussion by the researchers when it comes to reviewing weather forecasting models. ML uses a different approach for computing compared with the traditional or conventional programming paradigms. The traditional method follows step by step instructions to solve a problem while the ML enables a system to automatically learn and progress from experience without being explicitly programmed. Therefore, understanding the structure of the data and fit those data into human-understandable models are considered as the main goal of ML.

Machine learning (ML) provides a family of algorithms which enables the computer with the ability to automatically learn from experience and perform better by adapting to new situations [153]. The machine learning algorithms may be supervised, unsupervised, semi supervised or reinforcement. In supervised ML algorithms, models learn from the past labeled data and use it to generalize the new data [205]. In contrast, the unsupervised ML algorithms study the unlabeled data and try to draw inference rather than figuring out the correct output [206]. The semi-supervised ML algorithms use both labeled and unlabeled data and fall somewhere in between the above two learning methods. The reinforcement ML algorithms interact with the environment to learn the best action. As supervised learning algorithms analyze the past-labeled data to predict the unseen patterns, it suits to the problem of Weather forecasting. The accuracy is the most significant factor in weather forecasting. Moreover, it is feasible to create a training dataset with historical weather data which consists of both input and output data (i.e., labels). Therefore, the supervised ML models(using supervised algorithms) have been widely used in weather forecasting

[207].Besides, weather forecasting is a predictive analysis targeting on predicting continuous values. Therefore, regression ML algorithms are selected for this research.

Numerous machine learning methodologies are currently used for weather forecasting [46]. The most common methodologies are LR, Decision Tree, RFR, SVM, and ANN. These approaches can be combined with different approaches to improve the efficiency of models [208].

2.4.2 General Machine Learning Models

Neural network is a small computing network model in which each neuron takes a vector of input values and produces a single output value. Logistic regression is also called as model with minimal neural network. It is technically a neural network with a single hidden layer. The logistic regression model can be defined in two words such as logistic and regression [209].

The decision tree is another simple and extensively used supervised machine learning approach used for classification and regression tasks, the nodes illustrate the decision characteristics, the branches illustrate the probable results from the nodes, and the leaves explain the classes [210]. Every single parent node should have at least one child node in the decision tree. The decision tree algorithms are used to handle both classification (classification trees) and regression (regression trees) problems. The decision tree is constructed by splitting the source dataset, constituting the root node of the tree, into the successor children. The dataset splitting is based on a set of rules based on classification features. The main limitation of decision tree is it is highly sensitive to over fitting problem and node overlapping is there. However, this is reduced in random forest classifier, which constitute ensemble of decision trees for classification.

Random Forests (RF) is the most famous techniques in information mining. Multiple Decision Trees are built in a random fashion and in vast manner during the training time, gives us the impression like a forest and the class is predicted by considering the mode of the classes. It's an algorithm for guided ensemble learning. The Random Forest Tree takes a group of poor learners and combines them to build a stronger classification predictor. To put it another way, it's a random forest made up of decision trees (weak learners) (strong predictor). The random forest tree's main

42

purpose is to use a learning algorithm to merge numerous base level predictors into a single effective and resilient predictor. The forest classifiers are fitted with two arrays, one with training data and the other with the goal values of the testing data, while creating the random forest tree. Leo Breiman and Adele Cutler [211] invented the Random Forests calculation.

Support Vector Machine (SVM) is the most popular statistical learning concept based supervised machine learning technique that is defined using an optimal separating hyper plane, which can be used for machine learning applications such as classification and regression [212]. The vectors (training data) that define the hyper plane are called support vectors. The SVM technique was used in various extents, such as image, numerical, and text classification and regression applications. SVM techniques rely on a collection of mathematical functions known as the kernel. The kernel's job is to take data and turn it into the format that is needed. Different types of kernel functions are used by different SVM algorithms [213]. The most common kernel functions are linear, nonlinear, polynomial, and sigmoid. The SVM technique takes a long training time on massive datasets than other machine learning algorithms.

Artificial Neural Network is defined as an information management model that is identical to the function of biological nervous system of the human brain [214] which acts as an information processing machine. Thus, ANNs can handle complex non-linear time varying real-world problems like man's brain which can compute a variety of complex signals. ANN can be classified into Feedforward Neural Network (FFNN) and Recurrent Neural Network (RNN). Feedforward neural networks follow the principle of unidirectional information flow from input layer to output layer with no back-loops whereas recurrent neural networks do not have a restriction regarding back-loops. ANNs are self-adaptive data driven nonlinear models that try to simulate the structural components and underlying functionalities of the biological neural network. In order to do so, the basics of ANN are kept same to that of biological neural network. The simulation of biological neural network starts with its basic processing element i.e., "neuron". Equivalent to the components of biological neuron such as dendrite, soma, and axon, the artificial neuron has inputs, weights, bias, a summation unit, a transfer (activation) function and an output unit. In biological neuron, the information is input to the neuron through dendrites; soma processes it and produces the output through axon. Similarly, in artificial neuron, the information

43

is input to the neuron through weighted links. Then, it computes the weighted summation of inputs and "processes" the computed sum with a transfer function to produce the output.

Limitations of Machine Learning Models

Artificial intelligence and machine learning methods are preferred for data analytics nowadays for the reason of handling real-time data which is non-linear effectually.

Machine learning models are built upon statistical framework, implemented as supervised and unsupervised algorithms. The following are the issues faced by machine learning models in general in trying to forecast the events:

Time Series Issues: Unlike traditional prediction methods, time series forecasting adds on time component along with parameters used for forecasting. Hence the model must be able to incorporate the trend and seasonal pattern to the level component of every parameter correlated with forecasting. Most of the machine learning algorithms is developed based on classification problems but a different algorithmic approach is required for forecasting.

Those models which perceive the ability to incorporate the foregoing states for predicting the succeeding outcomes are well suited for time series analysis. Recurrent neural networks are one among such models for handling time series forecasting.

Lack of Quality Data: Machine learning algorithms need sufficient data to train the model, for example at least 10 years of data for time series forecasting. The input must be in fixed time intervals and aligned [215] based on time. Missing values and erroneous training data will propagate the error into the forecasting variable. Also, data are expected to be a more granular level for better pattern learning whereas aggregation tends to favor macro-level learning. If the data pattern changes abruptly, there may be a high deviation in the forecast from the actual outcome.

Accuracy Concern: Even though machine learning models are effective, they strive to attain the accuracy equivalent to statistical methods for forecasting. The reasoning behind is future errors, heterogeneous types of series, over-fitting in critical and inadmissible preprocessing [103]. Hence it is suggested to learn about unknown future errors by depersonalizing the data, clustering the data into different categories of series, introducing the condition to break off the optimization process to avoid over-fitting and to opt necessary transformation and trend removal. Another major concern is that the model must be trained for a change in data values every time and may not produce the same accuracy for test data.

Lack of Interpretability: Lack of transparency in internal logic and inner working of a model causes serious pitfalls as it prevents the experts to understand the reasoning and verify the decision made by the system [104]. Interpretability is the main inducement for the success of any artificial intelligence and machine learning system. Based on the degree of understanding why the decision was made by the system, a human can interpret the reason for prediction. Interpretability is also a cardinal reason for many researchers yet to adapt to statistical methods in various applications.

Stochastic Not Deterministic: Many machine learning models focus on probability measures for prediction. So, they do not follow any physical constraint like the acceptable values for the parameters used for forecasting. For example, rainfall value cannot be negative. So, research focus on enumerating physical constraints in machine learning models will minimize the supplementary executions in prediction and integrate the predicted values for further analysis.

2.4.3 Deep Learning

Deep learning (DL) is one of the recent areas in Machine Learning. It, a subset of Machine Learning (ML) methods and further ML is a subset of artificial intelligence. DL techniques achieved sound performance in several areas like automatic navigation systems, sentiment analysis, speech recognition and pattern matching [216][217]. DL techniques perform feature selection and training by constructing many hidden layers, apart from input and output layer. Therefore, DL techniques achieve good results compared to ML techniques [218][219]. Research proposed by G.E. Hinton in 2006 [220], which attempts to model data by combining different non-linear system with complex architecture. Deep machine learning is the subfield of ML in which learning methods are performed based on the data representation or feature learning. In deep learning system, set of methods are used to allow the system to discover the representation automatically required for feature detection or classification process from the raw data. Figure2.2 shows the process of Deep Learning. Neural Networks are the set of algorithms used in ML to perform complex mapping from the input to

45

the output. Neural networks have the ability to provide the training on supervised and unsupervised learning.

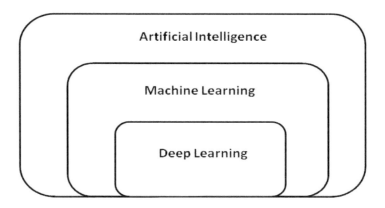

Figure 2.2 Deep Learning Process

A deep learning network is basically an artificial neural network, composed of multiple hidden layers in between the input and output layers. It could even accept raw data as input and generate appropriate feature representation with different levels of abstraction at each hidden layer [221].

Deep learning (DL) permits the computational frameworks that have multiprocessing layers to learn depictions of data with multiple abstraction levels. It is a sort of ML that facilitates computers to learn as of experience and comprehend the world grounded on a hierarchy of concepts. As the computer takes knowledge as of experience, a human-computer operator is not needed to formally signify all of the knowledge needed by the computer. The hierarchy of concepts permits a computer to effectively learn difficult notions by developing them as of simpler concepts; a graph of those hierarchies is several layers deep.

In deep learning model, the training dataset is the set of instances, and these instances are fed to the particular classifier for training the model. As the solutions to the input instances are already known, the deep learning classifier acquires the knowledge during training process for classifying the data into a particular class so that it could give the expected outputs and the training accuracy. The testing dataset is a collection of samples used to test the neural network and see how effectively it learns to classify data from the training dataset. Because the answers to these inputs are already known, the neural network is evaluated on these examples to see if it's making the expected predictions, even though it's been tested on new data that isn't part of the training dataset.

Figure2.3: Trend of 'Deep Learning' on Google (image Reference ("Google Trends," n.d.)).

Deep learning has been used in a variety of domains over the past ten years with remarkable results in terms of accuracy. The Google Trends graphs in Figure 2.3 shows that the attention drawn by deep learning approach during the last ten years (From October 2009 to October 2019). The Y-axis represents the search interest relative to the highest in the chart (i.e., the value 100 is the peak popularity), and X-axis represents the Year.

One of the key advantages of deep learning, as shown in Figure 2.4, is that learning algorithms can incrementally learn high-level features from data, eliminating the need for domain experts and hard-core feature extraction. In contrast, a domain expert needs to identify most of the applied features of the traditional ML to reduce the complexity of the data and make patterns more visible for the learning algorithms. Subsequently, deep learning works towards solving a problem end-to-end while ML will breakdown the problem statement into different parts, solve them individually, and combine the results at the end.

47

Machine Learning

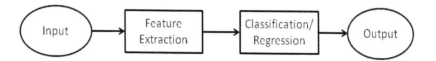

Deep Learning

Figure 2.4 Feature extraction: Machine learning vs. Deep learning.

Recent days, deep learning methods are doing impressive performance in various applications [222] across multiple datasets including weather prediction which are not needed to provide with the pre-defined features, but it can learn the features from the dataset itself [223]. Deep learning methods that contain many networks such as Artificial Intelligence, Machine Learning, Deep Learning, Convolution Neural Networks (CNN), Recursive Neural Networks, Recurrent Neural Networks (RNN) and Deep Belief Networks (DBN) used to perform the learning process effectively.

The Deep learning methods includes the enhanced software engineering, improved learning procedures and accessibility of computational power and training data [224] which are motivated by neuro science and achieved better impact in different applications such as NLP and Computer vision [225].

The way of learning the structure of model, layers quantity and the quantity of hidden variables in each layer are the basic challenges in Deep learning research. When dealing with different functions, the architecture of Deep learning provides full potential and labeled samples of high amount of raw data captured by the Deep architecture. The techniques of Deep learning networks have been developed in different fields such as object categories, navigation of robot, visual classification, acoustic signals, and time series prediction tasks. In the field of data, deep learning put more efforts to learn high level abstractions by extracting the hierarchical architectures. Deep learning approach is widely applied in the field of Artificial Intelligence. Recent days, deep learning is one of the successful leaning approaches, because of the three important reasons such as improve the abilities of chip processing, lower cost of hardware and significant improvement in ML algorithms [226][227]. Besides, a deep learning approach is capable of solving a problem end to end, able to learn high-level features from data in an incremental manner, eliminate the need of domain expertise, hard-core feature extraction, and takes less forecasting time compared to the traditional machine approaches even though the training time is high. Besides, it is practicable to produce larger labeled training datasets with historical weather data. The deep learning approach is selected for this research due to the benefits and adaptive nature,

2.4.4 General Deep Learning Models

There are three main deep learning architectures, namely Unsupervised Pretrained Networks (UPNs), Convolutional Neural Networks (CNNs), and Recurrent Neural Networks. UPNs is based on Unsupervised learning therefore is not considered to be discussed here. The CNN accepts fixed-size inputs, generates fixed size outputs, and originally designed with recognized images/video. In addition, a two-dimensional squared sliding window is used in the CNNs along an axis and convolute to identify patterns (i.e., convolute with the original two-dimensional image to identify patterns). Therefore, CNNs are ideal for images and classification problems in ML [228][229]. As described earlier, the classification category is not ideal for weather forecasting. Therefore, CNNs are not discussed further. Although, researchers like Zaremba et al.[230], have identified a prominent theme that deep learning models hold a complex set of sequences, RNNs are capable of handling arbitrary input/output lengths and use their internal memory to process an arbitrary sequence of inputs. These algorithms are originally designed to recognize sequences (or designed to work with sequence prediction) such as natural language processing and can be used for both classification and regression problems [231]. The internal memory units allow learning and generalizing across sequences of inputs rather than individual patterns. In RNN, each neuron may pass its signal latterly in a given layer, forward to the next layer, and the output may feedback as an input to the network with the next input vector. Therefore, RNNs can learn broader abstractions from the input sequences by adding state or memory to the network. A series of data which are indexed in time order is called as

49

the time-series data. Furthermore, data that represents a state in time can be called as the temporal data. RNNs are ideal for time-series information [232]. Because Time series data capturing the information of weather comprises of real numbers, regression techniques are frequently used to create and assess NN models for the prediction of accurate weather. [233]. Therefore, the RNN is selected for this predictive analysis research. There are two major issues to address the typical RNNs, namely 1) train the network with backpropagation and 2) gradient vanishing or exploding during the training [232]. In deep neural networks, propagation refers to the forward transfer of the signal of the input data through its parameters to make a decision. Backpropagation refers to altering the parameters in reverse through the network to minimize information about the error [234]. Therefore, the deep network first guesses about data using its parameters, then the network measure performance with a loss function, and finally the error adjusts the wrong-headed parameters with backpropagation. The recurrent or loop connections are breaking down the backpropagation process in RNNs creating a major issue [232][234].The gradient is calculated in RNNs to update the weights of the network [235]. This gradient tends to get much smaller on moving backwards into the network (i.e., in the backpropagation process) resulting in the neurons of the earlier layers learn very slowly as compared with the neurons of the layers appear in the later part of the hierarchy. This is called the gradient vanishing or exploding during the training process and results in taking much longer time by the network training process and decrease in the prediction accuracy of the model [236]. The earlier layers in a deep neural network work as basic building blocks as they are responsible for learning and detecting simple patterns. The next layers and the complete network do not work towards in producing accurate results if the earlier layers give improper and inaccurate results [236]. As a solution for the issues related with training the network with backpropagation and the vanishing gradient problem in RNNs, German researchers Sepp Hochreiter [115] has introduced a variation of RNN called LSTM in 1997. The LSTM allows recurrent nets to continue learning over many steps by maintaining a more constant error. Gated cells are used in LSTM to contain information outside the normal flow of the RNN where information can be stored, written to, or read from a cell much similar to the data in the computer memory [237]. Therefore, these gated memory blocks that are connected into the layers work as neurons. Compared to the classic neuron, each block has three gates that make it smarter, such as 1) The forget gate determines what

50

information should be discarded. 2) Input gate - determines which input values to update. 3) Output gate: determines what to output based on input and memory. As a result, in LSTM networks, each gated cell functions as a mini-state machine, with the gates of the units having weights learned during the training phase [238]. The RNN iterative process of making guesses, backpropagation error, and adjusting weights via gradient descent allows the cells to learn when to allow data to enter, leave or be deleted [237] . Consequently, the LSTM allows creating a large stacked recurrent network to address the complex problems in ML and achieve state-of-the-art-results. Therefore, the LSTM networks are used in many complex real-life applications such as text generation, handwriting recognition, music generation, language translation, and image captioning [239]. Weather forecasting is a complex process due to the chaotic nature of the atmosphere [204]. Moreover, the LSTM can overcome major issues with the RNNs. Therefore, the deep learning with LSTM approach is proposed for the fine-grained weather forecasting model in this research. In addition to the LSTM deep neural approaches, the Bi-directional LSTM has taken considerable attraction since its initial induction in 2001 for time series data [240]. Data are preserved from inputs that have already passed through the LSTM networks using its hidden state (i.e., the LSTM only preserves the information of the past). In contrast, the Bi-LSTM networks will run inputs in two ways, namely from the past to the future and from the future to the past. That is, the Bi-LSTM can run the inputs backwards to preserve information from the future when compared with the LSTM networks [241][242][243]. Therefore, the Bi-LSTM can preserve information from both past and future using the combined two hidden states. This process is helped by Bi-LSTM for a better understanding of the context. Thus, it targets a more accurate forecast compared to the LSTM networks in sequence-to-sequence applications (i.e. it knows the full inputs at prediction time) [244]. The RNN becomes the default choice for sequence modelling due to their superior ability to capture temporal dependencies in sequential data. Specifically, the LSTM has taken considerable attraction due to its great ability to capture long term dependencies [138].

Some of the important state-of-the-art ML and DL based models for weather forecasting and their merits and demerits are discussed in Table 2.2.

Table 2.2: Merits and demerits of existing machine learning and deep learning weather forecasting approaches.

Machine and Deep learning-based weather forecast techniques	Input/output parameters	Merits	Demerits
Modelling and forecasting the daily maximum temperature using abductive ML (Abdel-Aal and Elhadidy, 1995) [245] (Machine learning)	Input: Temperature, Wind Speed, Wind Direction, Pressure, Humidity. Output: Daily Maximum Temperature	Considerably reduced the computational requirements compared to NWP. Faster and highly automated model. Improved prediction accuracies compared to statistical forecasting models. Suitable for long-term prediction	Can use to predict single output parameter. Not suitable for area specific weather forecasting. Needs a greater understanding of the model before use.
ANN based Snowfall and rainfall forecasting from weather radar images (Ochiai et al., 1995) [246] (Machine learning)	Inputs: Snowfall and Rainfall. Outputs: Snowfall and Rainfall	Accurate compared to traditional cross correlation methods. 10 percent less computational training time compared to tradition ANN methods. Can be used to area specific or regional forecasting.	Limited to predict a single parameter at a time. Complex model. Limited to short-term forecasting
Rainfall estimation using M-PHONN model (Qi and Zhang, 2001)[247](Machine learning)	Input: Cloud Top Temperature, Cloud Growth, and Rainfall. Output: Rainfall	Increased speed and accuracy compared to traditional ANN. Ideal for very short time rainfall forecasting. Can be used for short-term forecasting with limited accuracy.	Not suitable for area specific weather forecasting. Requires satellite data to process Complex model
Intelligent weather monitoring systems using connectionist models (Maqsood et al., 2002) [248] (Machine learning)	Input: Daily Maximum, Daily Minimum Temperature, and Wind Speed. Output: Daily Maximum, Daily	Accurate forecasting compared to ELNN and MLP. Suitable for very long term forecasting. Able to predict all three parameters at once using the same	Not suitable for area specific weather forecasting. High model complexity. The accuracy decreases exponentially if the

Machine and Deep learning-based weather forecast techniques	Input/output parameters	Merits	Demerits
	Minimum Temperature, and Wind Speed	model.	number of days increases.
An efficient weather forecasting system using ANN (Baboo and Shereef, 2010) [249] (Machine learning)	Input: Pressure, Temperature, Humidity, Wind Speed, and Wind Direction. Output: Temperature	Short-term and long-term forecasting both can possibly be used. Accurate Short-term forecasting. Reduced Model complexity.	Limited to single parameter prediction. As the time difference between now and the anticipated time grows, the forecast becomes less reliable. Execution is time-consuming.
A rough set-based fuzzy neural network algorithm for weather prediction (Li and Liu, 2005) [250] (Machine learning)	Input: Dew Temperature, Wind Speed. Output: Dew Temperature, Visibility and Wind-Speed	Can use a single model to predict four parameters. Accurate short-term or medium-term forecasting. Suitable for area-specific weather forecasting	Complex algorithm. Not suitable for long term forecasting. Needs a greater understanding of the model before use. Need specific equipment to measure the input due temperature.
DNN based ultra-short-term wind forecasting (Dalto et al., 2015) [251] (Deep learning)	Input: Wind Output: Wind	It outperforms shallow ones. Can be used for regional or localized wind forecasting.	Limited to Short-term forecasting. Can use to predict single output parameter. Complex model.
Weather forecasting using DL techniques (Salman et al., 2015) [145] (Deep learning)	Input: Rainfall Output: Rainfall	Accurate RNN based forecasting results compared to Conditional Restricted Boltzmann Machine (CRBM), and Convolutional Network (CN) models. Faster execution time	Limited to short-term forecasting. Vanishing gradient issue. Use to predict a single output parameter

Machine and Deep learning-based weather forecast techniques	Input/output parameters	Merits	Demerits
Short-term local weather forecast using dense weather station by a DNN (Yonekura et al., 2018a) [252] (Deep learning)	Input: Temperature, Humidity, Pressure, Wind, and Rain. Output: Rain or Temperature	Compared to SVR and RF, yield the maximum accuracy for rain prediction (RF). Up to an hour of data prediction accuracy. Obtain input data from local weather stations.	Limitation of very short-term forecasting. Limited to predict single weather parameter at a time (either rain or temperature). High model complexity
Convolutional LSTM Network: A ML Approach for Precipitation Nowcasting (Shi et al., 2015)[253](Deep learning)	Input: Precipitation Output: Precipitation	Suitable for area-specific forecasting. Outperformed the fully connected LSTM approach. No vanishing gradient issue.	Limited to single output prediction. Not suitable for regional forecasting.
Nevada weather forecasting: A DL approach (Hossain et al., 2015) [144] (Deep learning)	Input: Pressure, Humidity, Temperature, and Wind Speed. Output: Temperature	able to predict accurate long-term temperature. Able to use for area specific temperature forecasting.	Limited to single output parameters. Not applicable for the forecasting of very short-term temperature.
LSTM Recurrent Neural Networks based Sequence to Sequence Weather Forecasting (Akram and El, 2016) [237] (Deep learning)	Input: Temperature, Humidity, and Wind Speed. Output: Temperature, Humidity, and Wind Speed	Forecast general weather variables with reasonable accuracy up to 24 hours compared to the ground truth. Suitable for regional forecasting.	Limited to predict a single output parameter at a time. Complex model. Not suitable for area specific weather forecasting.

Machine and Deep learning-based weather forecast techniques	Input/output parameters	Merits	Demerits
A DL Based on Bidirectional Gated Recurrent Unit for the prediction of Wind Power (Deng et al., 2019) `[254] (Deep Learning)	Input: Wind Speed and Wind Direction. Output: Wind Power	up to 6 hours wind power prediction. Suitable for both area specific and regional wind power forecasting.	The output contains a single parameter. Considerable time consuming to train the network compared to LSTM.

As per information from Table 2.2, different authors have used various machine learning and deep learning models independently or the combination of one or more machine learning and deep learning models with different input parameters like pressure, temperature, wind speed, dew point, rainfall, snow, and humidity. Every model has their own merits and demerits and most of the existing approaches either used one or less than or equal five inter-related input parameters for the NN based model of weather forecasting. A full AI-based model for weather forecasting with several additional weather parameters has yet to be investigated.

2.5 Analysis of Existing Deep Learning Weather Forecasting Models

As shown in Table 2.3, the differences and contributions of the existing deep learning weather forecasting models are compared. Merits and demerits of the existing state-of-the-art Machine learning and Deep learning approaches are discussed in Table 2.2 in Section 2.3. A model is proposed, based on the performances of these models, to solve the regression problem involving fine-grained weather forecasting models for a community of users in a specific domain.

Table 2.3: Existing deep learning weather forecasting models, their contributions, and drawbacks

Deep Learning Model	Model Description, Contribution, and Analysis	Drawbacks
Ultra-short-term wind forecasting model (Dalto et al., 2015) [251].	Contributed to a deep neural network for weather forecasting which outperformed the shallow ones compared to the MSE values. High accuracy wind forecast compared to shallow networks. Regional or area-specific forecast.	Single input and a single output parameter. Able to predict the wind parameter for less than 1-hour. Higher computational complexity compared to shallow neural networks. Not considered interrelated parameters.
Deep neural network rainfall prediction model (Hernández et al., 2016) [255].	Contributed to an architecture based on Deep Learning rainfall prediction model which outperformed the multi-layer perception ML models. Higher accuracy rainfall forecast based on MSE. Area-specific forecast up to 24 hours.	Single input and a single output. Not applicable for regional weather forecasting. Results may not be accurate as the observations of the interrelated parameters are not considered
RNN short-term forecasting model (Salman et al., 2015) [145].	Contributed to deep learning RNN for weather forecasting which outperformed CRBM and CN networks. High accuracy rainfall forecast compared to CRBM, and CN based on MSE values. Area-specific short-term forecast	Uses only single input and predicts a single output. High memory consumption compared to the CRBM, and CN based models. Applicable only for 6-hour forecast. Not considered the interrelated parameters
Deep neural network short-term forecasting model (Yonekura et al., 2018b) [252].	Contributed to a deep model which outperformed the SVR, and RF compared to MSE values. Higher accuracy rain and temperature forecasting compared to SVR and RF. Predict one parameter at a given time. Area-specific forecasting. Five inputs and single-output (Multi-input Single-output).	Predict only a single output parameter at a time. Able to predict forecast for less than 1-hour. Not applicable for regional forecasting. High computational complexity compared to SVR and RF. Vanishing gradient issue during the training process.

Deep Learning Model	Model Description, Contribution, and Analysis	Drawbacks
LSTM multilayered weather forecasting model (Salman et al., 2018) [256].	Contributed a comparison study of single-layer and multi-layer LSTM models for weather forecasting. The results show that the multi-layer LSTM yields accurate prediction compared to the single-layer ones. Accurate humidity, dew point, temperature, and pressure forecast compared to the ground truth and based on MSE. Regional or area-specific MISO based forecasting.	High computer complexity in multi-layer LSTM models compared to the single-layer models. Requires specific hardware such as GPU memory units for a productive output. In the case of a long input sequence, saving partial results for their various cell gates consumes a lot of memory.
Precipitation nowcasting model (Shi and Dustdar, 2016) [257].	Contributed a convolutional LSTM Network and outperformed the fully connected LSTM approach for precipitation nowcasting. Accurate precipitation forecasting comparatively to the ground truth based on MSE values. Area-specific very short-term forecast.	Able to predict less than 1-hour forecast. Single input and a single output. Prediction might not accurate as interrelated parameters are not considered. Requires GPU memory units for a productive output. Not suitable for regional forecasting.
DNN based feature representation model (Liu et al., 2014) [176].	Contributed a DNN model which represents the features of the raw weather data layer by layer which outperformed the classical SVR. Highly accurate temperature, dew point, pressure and wind speed forecasting compared to SVR. Regional long-term forecast up to 24 hours. Four inputs and single output at a time (multi-input Single-output).	Not suitable for an area-specific weather forecast. Able to predict only a single output at a time. For a productive output, this model requires specific hardware such as GPU memory units. High computational complexity compared to SVR. Uses a large number of components whose purpose is not immediately apparent.
A deep neural network model for temperature forecasting (Hossain et al., 2015) [144].	Contributed a stacked auto-encoder deep learning model for weather forecasting. 97.97% accurate temperature forecast compared to the ground truth. MISO based Area-specific long-term forecast up to a month.	Able to predict a single output parameter at a time. Not suitable for regional forecasting. Uses up a lot of memory in storing partial results. Training process is not efferent and time-consuming.

Deep Learning Model	Model Description, Contribution, and Analysis	Drawbacks
Sequence to sequence weather forecasting model (Akram and El, 2016) [237].	To map sequences of weather values of the same length, the authors proposed multi-stacked LSTMs. Reasonably accurate temperature, humidity, and wind speed forecasting compared to the ground truth based on MSE values. MIMO based regional forecast up to 24 hours.	Not suitable for area-specific weather forecasting. Uses multiple cell gates due to the long input sequence and uses a lot of memory. It is recommended to use GPU memory units for faster output.
Bi-LSTM wind power forecasting model (Deng et al., 2019) [254].	For weather power forecasting, authors proposed bidirectional gated recurrent network. The model established precise relationship between the power and wind speed, wind direction compared to the ground truth based on the MSE values. MISO based Local or regional forecast.	Able to predict parameters for up to 6 hours. Uses only a single observational weather parameter and not considered the interrelated parameters for an accurate prediction. Recommended to use specific hardware such as GPU memory units for productive output.

Analyzing the Table 2.3 above, it is clear that both regional weather forecasting and area specific forecasting can use deep learning techniques. Each approach has its own disadvantages. In particular, Salman et al., (2015) [145], Yonekura et al., (2018) [252] and Liu et al., (2014) [176] outperformed the classic ML approaches with deep learning models. Besides, Akram and El, (2016) [237], Dalto et al., (2015) [251], Salman et al., (2015) [145]and Salman et al., (2018) [256] concluded their research that the deep neural networks outperformed the shallow ones in weather forecasting. Thus, deep neural networks are chosen for this study rather than shallow neural networks. In addition, all state-of-the-art deep models are discussed in Table 2.2 using fewer than five interrelated parameters. One of the contributions of this research is developing a complete weather forecasting model with few more input parameters.

In Table 2.3, there are three types of regression, some of which are multi-input and multi-output, some of which are multi-input and single-output, and some of which are single-input and single-output. All of these regressions can show state-of-the-art performances with deep learning approaches. It is based on two factors, namely previous observations and prior observations of interrelated parameters, to determine the prediction accuracy of any selected parameter [258]. Furthermore, parameters linked to previous observations can produce a more accurate prediction than parameters with a lower degree of correlation[259]. Therefore, SISO regression is not mainly considered within this study as the main goal is to get an accurate forecast. MIMO produces lower MSE values when compared with MISO [138] also Jiancheng Qin et al. [260] states that "Although the MIMO model structure is more complicated compared to the other three models, there is no guarantee that the MIMO model will produce the best forecasting results", therefore MIMO is also not considered. As a consequence, MISO model is considered to overcome the regression problem in our proposed work for weather forecasting.

2.6 Research Gap

From a broad survey on weather forecasting, it is clear that every model has its own merits and demerits, but certain issues can be addressed by improving the model without losing the originality of the method. ARIMA is a standard statistical method used for most of the prediction applications that compete equally with machine learning models but due to its univariate forecasting nature, DNN overrides it. The following issues are yet observed in the existing methods.

- Traditional ANN uses a gradient descent algorithm for back propagation and hence suffers from vanishing gradient problem.
- It does not have the memory to hold the previous states of time series data.
- Suffers from the local minimum problem for longer forecasting periods, thus needing a larger number of epochs for better prediction. This increases computational complexity.
- Prediction accuracy is good for any standard models like ARIMA, ANN during normal season but the accuracy goes down for the extreme seasons.
- Minimum 10 years of data is needed to learn the weather pattern by the prediction models but most of the existing work (except a few) does not use a sufficient period for study.

- Most of the existing approaches either used one or less than equals to five interrelated input parameters for the neural network-based weather forecasting model.
- Most of the existing approaches predict limited weather parameters as output which is not sufficient for complete weather forecasting.
- SISO and MIMO regression models produce lower MSE values when compared with MISO.

Hence, certain features in the weather forecast are considered as important which acts as the cause for the occurrence of above-listed challenges in the existing models. This review provided insight to explore the use of deep learning model to overcome some existing challenges by considering some important features for efficient weather forecast.

CHAPTER-3

GENERAL

METHODOLOGY

Chapter 3

General Methodology

The research approach goes through relevant information collection to prove or disqualify the work by following a systematic process and to manage the sharing of logical findings. This chapter explains the general methodology used for the proposed work given in Figure 3.1 below which depicts a systematic way to solve a problem. The goal is to provide the work plan of research. In which first step is to collect weather data, which is initially unclean and hence cannot be used without preprocessing, hence after the collection of data the preprocessing is required for data cleaning, selection of features and standardizing the data. Although, a number of models are capable of training the raw input related data, decline in the performance level can result with the increase in the number of variables. Therefore, it necessitates a feature selection so that the quantity of input variables can be decreased. Feature selection is an approach towards the selection of the best subset of variables amounting to the reduction in the input dimension as well. The purpose of feature extraction is to reach the highly representative input data. After preprocessing, clean data is obtained in a desired format and further can be categorized into training and testing data. The training dataset is utilized for training all the three models, that are ARIMA, CRNN and Hybrid_Stacked Bi-LSTM followed by performance analysis which is performed using three evaluation metrics that is Mean Square Error, Root Mean Square Error and Mean Absolute Error. At last, a comparative analysis is carried out based upon the performances of these models in order to derive the best suitable model for weather forecasting.

Besides, this chapter also discusses the implementation setup and hardware used for this work with different controls configured during the process of training.

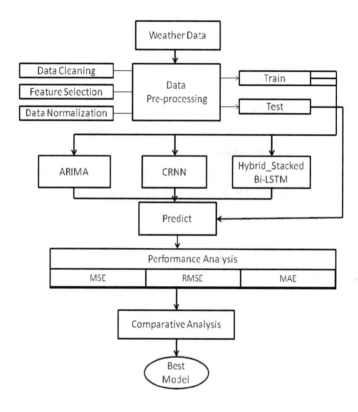

Figure 3.1: General Methodology

3.1 Dataset and Pre-processing

Weather data from Szeged, Hungry has been used for this study. Data set contains hourly weather data and it has 12 columns and 96453 rows. The attributes in the dataset are Time, Summary, Precipitation, Temperature, Apparent Temperature, Humidity, Wind Speed, Wind Bearing, Visibility, Loud Cover, Pressure and Daily Summary. Data set covers the time period between 2006 and 2016.

Source: https://www.kaggle.com/budincsevity/szeged-weather

Data Preparation

Data was generally inconsistent, inaccurate and having missing values so the gathered weather data are prerequisites to prepare before they can be used in neural network models so firstly we have to clean and interpolate the data to remove NULL values. 'Clean' means that there is no irrelevant data nor any labels, text, characters or symbols in the data. If there are any NULL values, these NULL values must be removed and data must be cleaned before they can be used with ML models. Therefore, removal of these NULL values and replacement by the arithmetic mean of the two adjacent vertical data items of the dataset (i.e. interpolating the dataset) is done. This is called linear interpolation and it can be achieved by using simple Python code.

After the dataset being linearly interpolated for the inclusion of missing values, the unnecessary columns which has only one or less unique values should be removed, because these parameters will not impact the training process. The next step is to find the correlations between parameters and highly correlated parameters should be removed. After that, all the non-numerical values present in our dataset should be converted to numerical values and for this 'LabelEncoder' is used that can be attained by the use of 'Sklearn' Library. 'Sklearn' comes up with a much efficient tool for the purpose of encoding the levels of categorical features into numerical values. After performing all these steps, all weather parameters are standardizing using Standard Scaler for the testing dataset to keep the values in a scale. It is not mandatory to standardize the independent data for neural networks in theory. But, relevant studies show that neural network training is often more efficient with standardized data and leads to a better prediction. .

Standard Scaler is a scaling method in which the values are centered on the mean with a unit standard deviation. As a resultant, the mean of the attribute becomes zero and the resultant distribution has a unit standard deviation. Following is the formula for standardization:

$$X' = \frac{X - \mu}{\sigma} \qquad\qquad (3.1)$$

Where σ is the standard deviation and μ is the mean of feature values. It is noteworthy that the numbers in this situation aren't limited to a specific range.

It is an important preprocessing step mainly performed prior to train various machine learning models so that standardization of the functionality range of the input dataset can be attained. It is used to perform Feature Scaling which is a phase of Data Preprocessing. Basically, it is used to scale the magnitude of the feature in a certain range. Generally, the data obtained from the real world have a great difference between them and have direct impact over the performance of the model. So, it's always a best practice to scale the data before processing it.

Given N features, Standard Scaler for each value in a particular feature can be calculated by:

$$\frac{\text{Value} - \text{Mean of Feature}}{\text{Standard deviation of Feature}} \qquad (3.2)$$

In Python, in order to avoid calculations, we have StandardScaler present in Sklearn package. StandardScaler for any dataset is generally calculated via functions available i.e fit_transform(dataset). We can use fit and transform functions separately. The fit function will calculate the mean and standard deviation whereas transform function will evaluate and replace the values. At last, the dataset is converted into daily data to train the models.

The predicted values are generated from the neural networks in the normalized format (i.e. input data are already in the normalized form). These data will be de-normalized and converted into the human-understandable format and then de-normalized data are used to compare the predicted results with the ground truth.

Eight relevant weather parameters in totality are extracted out of the daily dataset. Seventy percent of total dataset is utilized as a training dataset for training the models and rest 30 percent dataset is utilized for testing the models for the identification of the best model related to weather forecasting.

After performing all the necessary preprocessing steps, the details of our final dataset are depicted in Figure 3.2.

```
<class 'pandas.core.frame.DataFrame'>
DatetimeIndex: 4019 entries, 2005-12-31 00:00:00+00:00 to 2016-12-31 00:00:00+00:00
Freq: D
Data columns (total 8 columns):
 #   Column                 Non-Null Count  Dtype
---  ------                 --------------  -----
 0   Summary                4019 non-null   float64
 1   Precip Type            4019 non-null   float64
 2   Temperature (C)        4019 non-null   float64
 3   Humidity               4019 non-null   float64
 4   Wind Speed (km/h)      4019 non-null   float64
 5   Wind Bearing (degrees) 4019 non-null   float64
 6   Visibility (km)        4019 non-null   float64
 7   Pressure (millibars)   4019 non-null   float64
dtypes: float64(8)
memory usage: 282.6 KB
```

Figure 3.2: Details of preprocessed dataset

Historical weather data are time-series sequential data. Therefore, sequential data modelling techniques can be applied for these data to create and evaluate a fine-grained weather forecasting model.

3.2 Implementation Setup

There are quite a few model libraries that are used to enable neural networks and deep learning models in a computer system such as TensorFlow, BVLC, Theano, and Pfnetand. These model libraries are used as the backend of popular neural network models and each model library has its advantages and limitations while the most used is the TensorFlow backend. TensorFlow has a vast repository of data, however, it is complicated and not easy to use. Keras is a high-level Application Program Interface (API) and is more user-friendly. It allows rapid prototyping with a TensorFlow backend. Keras allows the building and testing of neural networks by reducing the lines of codes and has powerful APIs while its guiding principles are based on modularity. There are aspects like a sample, epoch, and batches are set so that data can be processed independently and distinctive phrases are identified. Therefore, the Keras API is selected for this research and the model is implemented using the Keras open-source neural-network tool using a Python environment.

65

Hardware Used

In this study, each experiment is carried out using general-purpose computers with Intel core i7 Central Processing Unit (CPU) having 3.4 GHz clock speed processor which has four cores, eight logical processors, and 32 GB physical Random-Access Memory (RAM). In addition to other basic configurations, these machines are comprised of 8 GB Graphical Processing Unit (GPU) memory.

3.3 Model Training

The process of finding the patterns in the training dataset that map the input data attributes to the target (i.e. the answer to predict or label) is called as model training [261]. In supervised learning, model training helps to determine the optimal values for all the 'weights' and the 'bias' form labeled input data [262]. There are different controls configured during this process, such as learning rate, optimizer, cost function, epoch, batch-size, and other deep network-related parameters.

Learning Rate (LR)

The LR is the most crucial hyper parameter followed by network configuration [263]. The 'how much to change the model' factor is controlled by the LR in response to the estimated error obtained each time the model weights are updated. If LR is too small, then the model requires a lengthy training process, and if it is too large, the results lead towards an unstable training process [264]. Therefore, it is quite challenging to arrange the learning rate in an ML model. To overcome this challenge, the LR scheduler is introduced for adjusting the LR at the time of training after decreasing it as per a pre-defined schedule [265]. There are three types of LR schedulers, namely, time-based decay, step-decay, and exponential-decay. In time based decay, the LR is updated by a decreasing factor in each epoch, and in step-decay, the LR drops by a factor for every few epochs. In exponential-decay, the LR is dropped exponentially for every epoch [266].

Optimizer

Optimizers are usually utilized in ML networks to minimize a given cost function after the model parameters such as weights and bias values are updated. In simple terms, the model is shaped to its most accurate possible form by 'futzing' with the weights and the optimizers. Stochastic optimizers like Adam [267] and SGD [268] have a wide usage for solving the cost function in deep models [269].

Epoch

The term of an epoch can be defined as one complete presentation of the dataset to be learned during the model training process [270]. Many epochs are used in learning machines such as feedforward neural networks that use iterative algorisms during the learning phase [115]. Therefore, the epoch is a measure which determines the number of times the training dataset is used once it is got to update the weights [261].

Number of Samples and Batch Size

It is well known that the sample is a single row of data in a dataset. Therefore, several samples can be defined as the total number of samples (i.e. total number of rows) in a dataset. In general, the training dataset comprised of many samples. The training dataset can be divided into one or more batches and the batch-size can be defined as the number of samples to propagate through before updating the internal model parameters. The popular batch sizes include 32, 64, 128, and 256. If the sample size is a lower figure, the training process uses less memory and is efficient.

Deep Network-Related Parameters

The model configuration is one of the key parameters related to the deep networks. This parameter defines the amount of layers in the deep network along with different amounts of nodes in every layer [232].

Models

The preprocessed weather data can be used to train various models. For the present work three different models have been taken in account i.e. ARIMA, CRNN and the proposed Hybrid_Stacked Bi-LSTM. Out of these ARIMA is a statistical model used for non-stationary time series data, represented by ARIMA (p,d,q) where p specifies the auto regressive order, d specifies the level of differencing while q specifies an order of moving average. ARIMA model forecasting process is dissimilar from other methods because it does not consider any particular pattern from the past data, but identifies a suitable model from the collection of models iteratively.

The remaining two are Deep learning models in which CRNN consists of single one dimensional convolutional layer and two LSTM layers. One dimensional convolutional layer is used to obtain lateral features from the time series data. LSTM layers are used to extract temporal features from the temperature time series.

The proposed Hybrid_Stacked Bi-LSTM network is formed by a combination of LSTM and Bi-LSTM. The proposed model comprises of three stacked LSTM layers and three Bidirectional LSTM layers.

As discussed in Section 2.5, multiple input single output (MISO) regression model is proposed for this research. For this, all of the weather parameters are provided to the network, then the network predicts a single parameter. Figure 3.3 depicts the necessary arrangement of the multiple input single output (MISO) models.

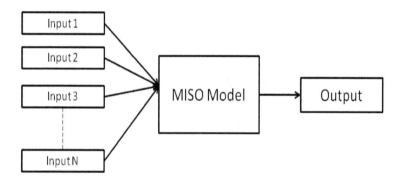

Figure 3.3: Proposed MISO model architecture

So, all the three models used in this study used MISO approach for forecasting. Further these three models are explained in the next three chapters, i.e. Chapter 4 for weather forecasting using ARIMA, Chapter 5 for weather forecasting using CRNN and Chapter 6 for weather forecasting using Hybrid_Stacked Bi-LSTM in detail.

3.4 Performance Analysis

Evaluating the performance of various models of the weather forecasting is a critical key component for forecasting system operations. Evaluation of each of the model should be done before the choice of the best model for the forecast.

The testing dataset is used to test the model performance in terms of accuracy. The model performance is the way to evaluate the solution to a problem. That is, the trained model is used to predict parameters and for comparing the results with the labels to calculate the model accuracy. The model accuracy could be calculated as a numerical figure in regression models and the common evaluation metrics are MSE, MAE, and RMSE.

After training of the model using three different methods, the performance of each model is analyzed using different parametric evaluation metrics i.e. Mean Square Error (MSE), Root Mean Squared Error (RMSE) and Mean Absolute Error (MAE) and is compared to determine the optimal model for weather forecasting as there are different models trained by different configurations and controls.

Mean Square Error (MSE)

Mean Square Error (MSE) is a measure of prediction accuracy. The lower Mean Square Error (MSE), the more accurate will be the predictions. It is also named as a standard squared error. It measures variance of forecast error. It's a measure of the anticipated values' average squared deviation. MSE provides a holistic picture of the predicting error. It panelizes the forecasting errors which were excessive. Changes in scale and data transformations lay an impact on MSE. It's a worthy measure of overall forecast error, nevertheless it isn't as intuitive or easily understandable as the other measures. The mathematical formulation is given as follows:

$$\text{MSE} = \frac{1}{n}\sum_{t=1}^{n}(Y_t - f_t)^2 \qquad (3.3)$$

Where,

Y_t= Actual values.

f_t = Forecast values

n = Number of forecasts

Root Mean Square Error (RMSE)

The Root Mean Square Error is a generally utilized metric for determining the difference between the model's predicted values and the actually observed values in the environment. Individual differences are referred to as residuals, and the RMSE is used to combine them into a single predictive power score. It's very useful when there are a lot of significant errors. By squaring the difference, it prevents the positive and negative deviations from cancelling each other.

Comparison of the RMSE between calculated and observed values provides a short-term evaluation of the correlation's performance. The smaller the value, the better the model performs, and RMSE is a non-systematic error. It is given by:

$$RMSE = \sqrt{\sum_{t=1}^{n} \frac{(e_t)^2}{n}} \qquad (3.4)$$

Where,

$e_t = Y_t - f_t$ =Forecast error

Y_t = Actual values.

f_t = Forecast values

n = Number of forecasts

Mean Absolute Error (MAE)

Mean Absolute Error (MAE) is a number that is used to calculate how similar the final results are to predictions. It gives the absolute value of bias error and is a measure of the goodness of correction. Essentially, it measures the absolute deviation between future forecasted values and actual ones. It measures the magnitude of forecasting error experienced in overall forecasting. In this case, positive and negative errors do not cancel out. It is important for a forecast to have as small and absolute error as possible, so the measurements and data transformations must be scaled accordingly. It is given by:

$$MAE = \frac{\sum_{t=1}^{n} |e_t|}{n} \qquad (3.5)$$

Where,

$e_t = Y_t - f_t$ =Forecast error

Y_t = Actual values

f_t = Forecast values

n = Number of forecasts

Table 3.1: Details of different evaluation metrics used

MSE/RMSE	MAE
Based on square of error	Based on absolute value of error
Value lies between zero to infinity	Value lies between zero to infinity
Perceptive to outliers, punishes larger error more	Target larger and small errors equally, not sensitive to outliers
Small value indicates better model	Small value indicates better model

After the performance analysis, a comparative analysis between all three models is performed in chapter 7 on the basis of above parametric evaluation metrics to find out the best suitable model for weather forecasting.

CHAPTER-4

WEATHER

FORECASTING USING

ARIMA

Chapter 4

Weather Forecasting using ARIMA

4.1 ARIMA Model

The ARIMA model was first developed during the early 1970s but Box-Jenkins developed appropriate systematic method in 1976. The acronym ARIMA stands for "Auto-Regressive Integrated Moving Average." The model comprises of three components i.e. Auto-Regressive, Integrated and Moving Average as shown in Figure 4.1. As per the forecasting equation, lags of the differenced series are called "auto-regressive" terms, lags of prediction errors are called "moving average" terms, and a time series that needs to be differenced and considered to be stationary is called a "integrated" version of a stationary series. This mathematical model follows a complex time series analysis model. Generally, in a time series model there is a linear relationship between the past and future values and linear regression models are the most preferred model for prediction as it is easy to predict values, furthermore it is simple to explain and also to implement these models [271]. The time series remains stationary if it is statically invariant. Time series that are stationary can be furthered modelled using different parameters [272]. However, time series that are not stationary are statistically difficult to predict even if the existing values are provided.

ARIMA mode can predict the weather in a limited period of time and for this analysis it requires a minimum of 50 observations [273]. Furthermore, ARIMA model uses error to measure the differences between estimation and observations.

Auto-Regressive models, Exponential smoothing models, Random-walk and random-trend models are all examples of ARIMA models (i.e. exponential weighted moving averages). An "ARIMA (p, d, q)" model is a non-seasonal model in which p represents the number of autoregressive terms, d represents the number of non-seasonal differences, and q represents the number of lagged forecast errors in the prediction equation. [274].

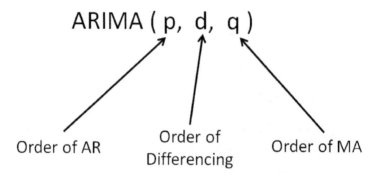

Figure 4.1: A General View of ARIMA models.

4.2 Forecasting Approach in ARIMA

A powerful classical model that combines Auto Regressive model and Moving Average model through a difference process "integrated" to make the series stationary is called an ARIMA model. An auto-regressive model of order 'p' is abbreviated as AR(p) and it is based on the past 'p' values of the variable Y_t .

Thus, if Y_t denotes the present value of the variable, it is expressed as a linear combination of its own preceding values at times t-1, t-2...t-q plus a random disturbance e_t . The following is the representation of an auto-regressive model of order 'p':

$$Y_t = b_0 + b_1 Y_{t-1} + b_2 Y_{t-2} + ... + b_p Y_{t-q} + e_t \qquad (4.1)$$

The above equation resembles a multiple regression model except that Y_t is regressed on its past values instead of different predictor variables, hence the prefix 'auto' in autoregressive model.

Similarly, MA (q) is the abbreviation for the moving average model of order 'q' and it is based on the past 'q' disturbances or prediction errors of the past values of the same variable. As a result past errors are used as explanatory variables in MA (q). Following is the representation of a moving average model of order 'q':

$$Y_t = b_0 + b_1 e_{t-1} + b_2 e_{t-2} + ... + b_p e_{t-q} + e_t \qquad (4.2)$$

73

As a result of efficient coupling of autoregressive model along with moving average model a general and efficient class of the time series model called ARMA is formed. And by differencing the data series this class of models can be extended as the ARIMA model for a non-stationary time series. Non-stationary data cannot be modeled or forecasted due to their unpredictability. In most time series problems, data will be non-stationary. It will be converted into stationary to obtain consistent and reliable results by doing differences by an order of integration parameter 'd'. The first differences are given by the equation,

$$(z_t - z_{t-1}) = (1-B)z_t \qquad (4.3)$$

The second differences which are obtained by finding the differences of first differences are given by the equation,

$$(z_t - 2z_{t-1} + z_{t-2}) = (1-B)^2 z_t \qquad (4.4)$$

Proceeding like this, in general the dth differences are given by $(1-B)^d z_t$

Thus, an ARIMA (p,d,q) model of the non-stationary behavior is of the form

$$\phi(B)(1-B)^d z_t = \theta(B) a_t \qquad (4.5)$$

Where observed value at time t is z_t, noise is denoted by a_t and the backward shift operator B is defined by

$$Bz_t = z_{t-1} \qquad (4.6)$$

$\phi(B)$ is the autoregressive operator of order 'p' and is defined by

$$\phi(B) = 1 - \phi_1 B - \phi_2 B^2 - \dots - \phi_p B^p \qquad (4.7)$$

$\theta(B)$ is the moving average operator of order 'q' and is defined by

$$\theta(B) = 1 - \theta_1 B - \theta_2 B^2 - \dots - \theta_q B^q \qquad (4.8)$$

There are some general rules for detecting the values of 'p' and 'q' from the ACF and PACF plots which determines the order of the ARIMA model. They are given as under:

- A gradual decay in the ACF plot and a sharp cut off in the PACF plot at lag 'k' suggests that the model is an autoregressive model of order 'k'.
- A gradual decay in the PACF plot and a sharp cut off in the ACF plot at lag 'k' implies that the model is a moving average model of order 'k'.

- A gradual decay in both ACF and PACF plots which starts after k_1th and k_2th lag for ACF and PACF respectively indicates that the model is an autoregressive moving average model of order (k1, k2).

Having made a good guess of the correct values of 'p' and 'q' using error measures, the correct model is fitted with these values. If the model is correct then the ACF and PACF plots of the residuals of the correctly identified model will not have any significant spikes (spikes are the vertical lines that extend beyond the horizontal dotted lines in the ACF and PACF plots) at the first few lags. After having found the correct model, it is fitted to a time series and has to be checked whether the model provides an adequate description of the data. If the values of 'p' and 'q' do not satisfy the stationary conditions, then one has to identify a new model for which the new parameters are estimated and tested. This process of finding the parameters, testing the parameters and then finalizing the parameters will make up the required model. Once the model is chosen, a forecast is done. This whole process of ARIMA methodology can be given in a crispy and short manner in the form of a flowchart. Thus, the flow chart for ARIMA Methodology is given in Figure 4.2.

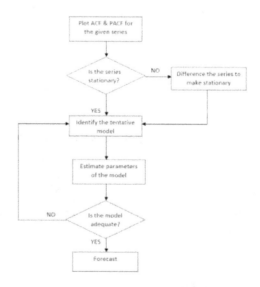

Figure 4.2: Flowchart of ARIMA Model

Seasonality means periodic fluctuations in a time series. It represents the existence of variations in a time series that occur in regular intervals less than a year like weekly, monthly, quarterly, half-yearly and so on.

The pattern that repeats itself over fixed interval of time is termed to be seasonality. The periodic pattern of period's that appears in the ACF plot shows the existence of a seasonal component of lengths. If seasonality is present in the time series, then it can be forecasted by a seasonal ARIMA model. From Figure4.3, Figure4.4, Figure4.5 and Figure4.6, it can be observed that the study of the research work involves daily data of Temperature, Wind Speed, Humidity and Rainfall respectively and hence seasonal variations do not exist.

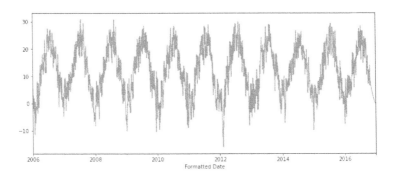

Figure 4.3: Time series plot of Temperature data

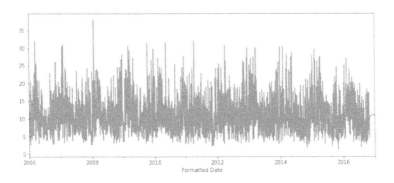

Figure 4.4: Time series plot of Wind Speed data

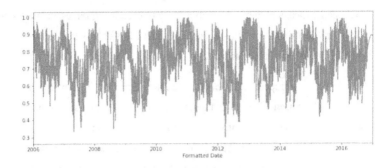

Figure 4.5: Time series plot of Humidity data

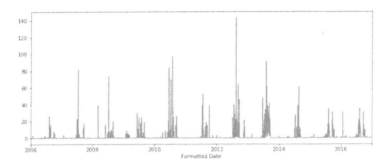

Figure 4.6: Time series plot of Rainfall data

Based on the flowchart given in Figure 4.2, firstly the weather data is plotted for all four parameter according to the time series. The time series plots of data are shown in Figure 4.3, Figure 4.4, Figure 4.5 and Figure 4.6. Then 'P' value needs to be calculated, which is basically a probability and it should be as small as possible. Ideally, it should be less than 0.5. If it is higher than 0.5 that means dataset is not stationary.

```
1. ADF :  -3.9904281476411927
2. P-Value :  0.0014614700044928118
3. Num Of Lags :  16
4. Num Of Observations Used For ADF Regression and Critical Values Calculation : 4002
5. Critical Values :
        1% :  -3.4319850573119437
        5% :  -2.8622624788783146
        10% :  -2.567154583183171
```

Figure 4.7: P value test of Temperature

```
1. ADF :  -14.128715197379224
2. P-Value :  2.3543421392475615e-26
3. Num Of Lags :  10
4. Num Of Observations Used For ADF Regression and Critical Values Calculation : 4008
5. Critical Values :
        1% :  -3.431982608051027
        5% :  -2.8622613969260846
        10% :  -2.5671540071976806
```

Figure 4.8: P value test of Wind Speed

```
1. ADF :  -6.438669472632128
2. P-Value :  1.628644159576389e-08
3. Num Of Lags :  14
4. Num Of Observations Used For ADF Regression and Critical Values Calculation : 4004
5. Critical Values :
        1% :  -3.4319842400755096
        5% :  -2.862262117867148
        10% :  -2.5671543909961168
```

Figure 4.9: P value test of Humidity

```
1. ADF :  -7.181515915104875
2. P-Value :  2.642347120274765e-10
3. Num Of Lags :  25
4. Num Of Observations Used For ADF Regression and Critical Values Calculation : 3993
5. Critical Values :
        1% :  -3.4319887450134567
        5% :  -2.862264107905561
        10% :  -2.567155450408488
```

Figure 4.10: P value test of Rainfall

From Figure 4.7, Figure 4.8, Figure 4.9 and Figure 4.10, it is clear that the 'p' value calculated for all four parameters is less than 0.5 hence indicates the data is stationary. After looking seasonality and randomness of the data and then ACF and PACF of the data were calculated, it is found that our data is stationary so the next step is to estimate our model to predict the best p, d, and q values for each parameter. Selection of the best fitted ARIMA model for the data, their goodness of fit was made through evaluation using the Akaike Information Criteria (AIC), AIC is an important and leading statistics by which the order of an autoregressive model can be determined. The AIC considers several parameters for the best fit and also the extent to which model is suitable for the best fit. The lowest AIC criterion values produced a selected model, which is positively closer to the best probable choice.

After applying various different combinations of p, d and q values the most appropriate model is determined with ARIMA(2,0.2) for temperature, ARIMA(1,0,3) for wind speed, ARIMA(5,0,4) for humidity and ARIMA(1,1,1) for rainfall because these combination gives minimum AIC. Finally, these selected models are applied for forecasting parameters respectively.

4.3 Results

As described in Section 3.1, the ARIMA model is trained with the training dataset. The testing dataset is used to get a prediction using the trained model. The prediction results are compared with the ground truth. The error figures are calculated for each parameter. ARIMA(2,0.2), ARIMA(1,0,3), ARIMA(5,0,4) and ARIMA(1,1,1) is considered as hyper parameter to forecast predicted values of temperature, wind speed, humidity, and rainfall respectively. The system executes a respective code for each parameter to analyze the ARIMA model. Each code predicted the weather for the appropriate parameter.

The predicted results of all four weather parameters are compared with the ground truth (actual values), and the evaluation results are shown in Table 4.1. Before comparison, the model prediction is de-normalized and converted to the human-understandable format. The reason for this is that the historical weather dataset used in this research is in real/actual values (i.e. not normalized nor in any other format) and is easy to understand. The proposed model is evaluated mainly using the MSE metric. While evaluating the results, there are some other metrics also employed such as MAE, RMSE. All of these evaluation metrics work in a similar manner to calculate the error. The values of these errors should be minimum for better performance of the model.

Table 4.1: Evaluation results for ARIMA model

Parameters	Evaluation Metrics		
	MSE	RMSE	MAE
Temperature	2.252	1.500	0.806
Wind Speed	4.964	2.228	1.700
Humidity	0.003	0.055	0.044
Rainfall	3.753	1.937	0.755

The value of all these evaluation metrics for ARIMA model is given in Table 4.1 shows the skills of the ARIMA for the forecasting of future weather data.

As there are 1197 samples in testing data, the ARIMA model will generate similar number of outputs as the predicted data. Because of the large sample size, it is difficult to visualize all of these predictions so the prediction results of all four parameters for the 1197 days are presented graphically. Figure 4.11, Figure 4.12, Figure 4.13 and Figure 4.14 displays the prediction results of temperature, wind speed, humidity and rainfall respectively where the blue line represents the ground truth (Actual) values for the particular day while orange line represents the prediction results for the corresponding day.

The prediction results of ARIMA will be compared with the results of deep learning models in Chapter 7 to determine the accuracy and suitability of the model

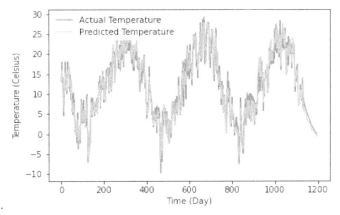

Figure 4.11: Graphical analysis of the actual and the predicted Temperature for ARIMA model

Figure 4.11 displays graphical analysis of actual temperature and predicted temperature for ARIMA model in which x axis is for Time (Day) and y axis is Temperature in Celsius.

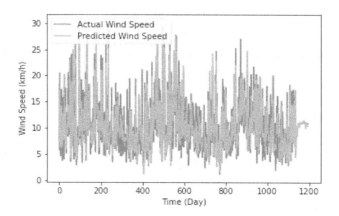

Figure 4.12: Graphical analysis of the actual and the predicted Wind Speed for ARIMA model

Figure 4.12 displays graphical analysis of actual wind speed and predicted wind speed for ARIMA model in which x axis is for Time (Day) and y axis is wind speed in km/h.

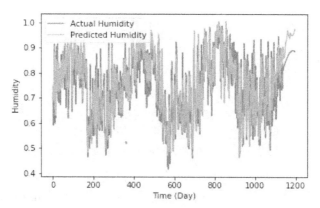

Figure 4.13: Graphical analysis of the actual and the predicted Humidity for ARIMA model

Figure 4.13 displays graphical analysis of actual humidity and predicted humidity for ARIMA model in which x axis is for Time (Day) and y axis is humidity in percentage.

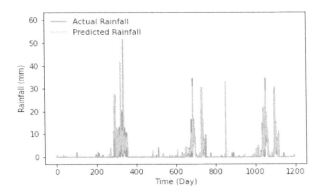

Figure 4.14: Graphical analysis of the actual and the predicted Rainfall for ARIMA model

Figure 4.14 displays graphical analysis of actual rainfall and predicted rainfall for ARIMA model in which x axis is for Time (Day) and y axis is rainfall in mm.

Advantages and limitations of the ARIMA model

ARIMA modelling has been highlighted as a valuable forecasting technique on numerous occasions. The ARIMA model's key advantage is that it produces results that are difficult to beat for short-term forecasts using high frequency data. They also have the advantage of being less sensitive than many other systems to the underlying assumptions regarding the nature of the data fluctuations. While the basic form can handle a wide range of functional forms, the exact form described must closely match the actual data. The ARIMA approach is only suited for a stationary time series (i.e., the autocorrelation, variance and mean are supposed to be nearly constant throughout time) and it is recommended that the input data include at least 50 observations. ARIMA models are typically expensive due to the significant data needs, deficient in available updating tools, and also the fact that their estimation is based on using non-linear estimating procedures. The estimated parameter values are also assumed to be constant throughout the series.

CHAPTER-5

WEATHER FORECASTING USING CRNN

Chapter 5

Weather Forecasting using CRNN

5.1 CRNN Model

This chapter presents the weather forecasting model CRNN, a combination of state-of-the-art deep learning models i.e. Convolutional Neural Network (CNN) and Recurrent Neural Network (RNN) to be used with historical weather data and thus target a more accurate forecast compared to the statistical models. Here LSTM is used which is a special type of RNN along with CNN. A one-dimensional convolutional layer extracts spatial characteristics, while LSTM layers extract temporal features in the deep learning model. This model is applied by analyzing the existing deep learning-based weather forecasting techniques discussed in Table 2.3 in section 2.5. The remaining sections of the chapter discusses the architecture of the CRNN model and how it can be used with the approaches of CNN and LSTM for the forecasting of weather and finally results obtained by the model.

5.2 Forecasting Approach in CRNN

The deep learning model CRNN presented in this work comprises of a single one-dimensional convolutional layer and two LSTM layers. These layers employ a set of coefficients to combine data and input, allowing them to perform computational tasks [232]. One dimensional convolutional layer is considered for time series prediction which is capable of extracting lateral features and capturing short-time connections from the time series data. LSTM layers are used to extract temporal features from the time series and are good at capturing long-time temporal characteristics. Figure 5.1 depicts the deep learning model with 1D-CNN and stacked LSTM layers for the MISO model.

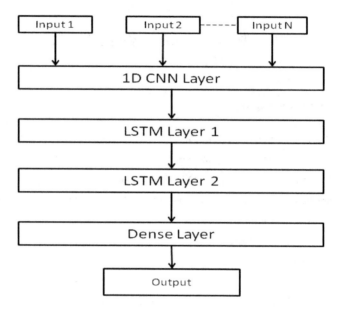

Figure 5.1: CRNN model

The number of layers and the number of memory cells in each layer is decided experimentally for the best performance. The CRNN model is a lightweight model that consists of a 1D CNN layer, LSTM layers and dense layer in addition to input and output layers. As discussed in Section 3.1, seven surface weather parameters are used as inputs for this model. This model provides outputs which is the predicted weather parameter.

One dimensional Convolution layer

CNNs (Convolutional neural networks) have evolved in recent years. Initially it was developed for the examination of long-range patterns using a hierarchy of temporal convolutional filters. The key characteristics of CNNs are: 1) it involves causal convolutions and 2) the network can accept any sequence of any length and map it to an output sequence of the similar length like in RNN; Convolution operation is a function which is derived from two given functions where it can be used express how the shape of one function can be modified by the other function. CNNs are trained using back propagation algorithm [30]. Furthermore, CNNs are commonly used for image processing related tasks. CNNs share similar properties and similar approach

84

without considering the dimensionality. But the main difference is from the input data dimensionality and the way filter slides across the given data. In a one dimensional convolutional layer filter slides alone a single dimension over the dataset and it will extract the highest level of feature. There are some specific features related to smaller filter sizes such as a smaller receptive field, the capture of smaller and more sophisticated features, and the ability to extract a vast amount of information, better computationally efficient, better weight sharing, and the requirement of significantly more memory. On the other hand, the larger filter sizes have specific features such as larger respective field, the capture of quite generic features, a higher number of internal weights and computationally expensive, easy to learn simple non-linear features, and a need for comparatively smaller memory. Therefore, both smaller filter sizes and larger filter sizes are investigated such as 32, 64, 128, 256, and 512. Our time series data set has seven dimensions they are time steps and parameter values. Therefore, filter or kernel can only move along the time dimension as shown in Figure 5.2.

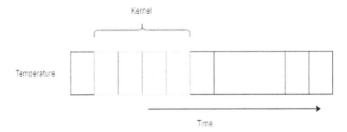

Figure 5.2: Kernel sliding over data

LSTM Layer

LSTMs (Long short term memory) were introduced by Hochreiter and Schmidhuber [115]. LSTM networks are a form of RNN (Recurrent neural networks) in which the initial low-cell neurons are replaced with cells with more sophisticated internal structures. Long-term dependencies can be learned by using LSTM's. For training, RNNs use truncated back propagation through time. However, if the number of time steps is very large, RNNs suffer from the vanishing gradient problem.

Due to memory units, LSTMs are capable of learning long term dependencies. They can also overcome vanishing gradient problem. The network can learn, forget previously concealed states, and update hidden states using these memory units. The cell state and numerous gates of LSTMs are updated. The general layout of an LSTM memory cell is shown in Figure 5.3.

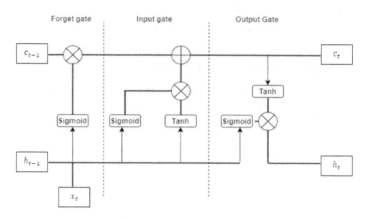

Figure 5.3: LSTM memory cell (image reference[232])

Forget gate: The forget gate's function is to figure out which memories should be erased. The sigmoid function is used to combine the information from the previous hidden state and the present input. If the value is near to 0, it indicates abandonment, and if it is close to 1, it indicates retention.

Input Gate: The responsibility of input gate is to update the cell state. The sigmoid function is applied to the prior hidden state and current input, it determines which values should be changed first. Where 0 indicates that no changes are required and 1 indicates that changes should be made. In order to change values between -1 and +1, a tanh gate is used. The output of these two gates' are multiplied and then added to the cell state.

Output gate: The output gate is responsible for determining the next hidden state. To determine which information should be included in the next hidden state, a sigmoid function is applied to the previous hidden state and the current input. The modified cell state is then subjected to the tanh gate. Multiplying these two gate values generates the next hidden state. [31].

Deep learning model CRNN have investigated with different configurations and controls. Each network configuration has a different number of layers and each layer consists of a different number of nodes. These configurations have experimented with different controls mainly learning rate and optimizer. In this work, to find out the best possible forecasting approach, a 1D CNN is used, which comprises of a single Convolutional layer. The following settings are used in the Convolutional layer: 64 filters, stride equal to 1, kernel size equal to 3, padding is set to "same" and Rectified Linear Unit 'relu' is used as activation function. LSTM network is also used with a single 1D CNN layer which consists of two stacked LSTM layers, out of which one layer is of 32 LSTM units and other is of 16 LSTM units, along with two fully connected layers. The number of neurons in the first fully connected layer is set to 8 which are further connected to a single neuron in the output layer and activation function used is Rectified Linear Unit 'relu'. The model gives the best value with Adam optimizer, batch size 256 and learning rate 0.0018. MSE cost function is selected to find the loss for experiments as this study is based on regression modelling, which is calculated as Equation 3.3. The least MSE is found at the 177 epochs for temperature, 340 epochs for wind speed and 198 epochs for humidity and 236 epochs for rainfall parameter.

The other obvious hyper parameter is data_dim=7 (i.e. the number of parameters in each timeslot), time steps=30, the shape of the training dataset (2792, 30, 7) where 2792 is the number of samples in the training dataset followed by time steps and data_dim.

5.3 Results

As described in Section 3.1, the CRNN model is trained with the training dataset and testing dataset is used to get a prediction using the trained model. The prediction results are compared with the ground truth for all four parameters. As described in Section 5.2, the model is evaluated with several configurations and controls to find an optimal model with least MSE and 'save the best model' approach is used while training the model. In this case, the system checks the loss function value for each epoch with the saved model. Only if the new loss value was smaller than the saved model loss, the system saved the new model as the best model. The saved best model is used to get the prediction for the testing dataset and evaluate the results with respect to the ground truth. The model is evaluated mainly using the MSE metric. While evaluating the results, there are some other metrics also employed such as MAE, RMSE. All of these evaluation metrics work in a similar manner to calculate the error. The values of these errors should be minimum for better performance of the model. In a practical situation, the values of some weather parameters can be zero. Some examples are rain and even temperature. This is one of the main reasons the regression modelling prefers to use averages to calculate the errors, such as MSE, MAE, and RMSE.

Table 5.1 present the best MSE, RMSE and MAE values for all four parameters. This evaluation is carried out using the actual values and not the normalized data (i.e. the normalized predictions are converted to the human-understandable form and compared with the actual ground truth values).

Table 5.1: Evaluation results for CRNN model

Parameter	Evaluation Metrics		
	MSE	RMSE	MAE
Temperature	1.368	1.169	0.890
Wind Speed	2.706	1.645	1.256
Humidity	0.001	0.042	0.034
Rainfall	1.369	1.170	0.469

The values of all these evaluation metrics for the CRNN model is given in Table 5.1 shows the skills of the CRNN model for forecasting future weather data.

As there are 1197 samples in testing data, the CRNN model will generate similar number of outputs as the predicted data. Because of the large sample size, it is difficult to visualize all of these predictions so the prediction results of all four parameters for the 1197 days are presented graphically. Figure 5.4, Figure 5.5, Figure 5.6 and Figure 5.7 displays the prediction results of temperature, wind speed, humidity and rainfall respectively where the blue line represents the ground truth (Actual) values for the particular day while orange line represents the prediction results for the corresponding day.

The prediction results will be compared with the results of other models in Chapter 7 to determine the accuracy and suitability of the model.

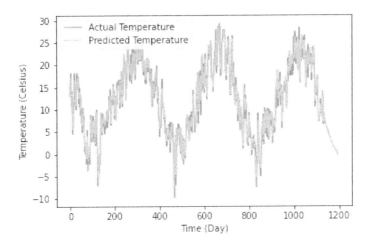

Figure 5.4: Graphical analysis of actual v/s predicted Temperature for CRNN model

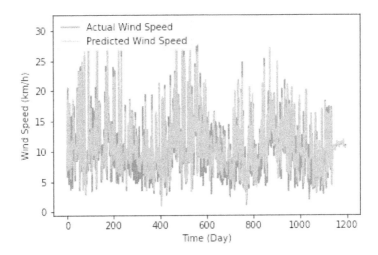

Figure 5.5: Graphical analysis of actual v/s predicted Wind Speed for CRNN model

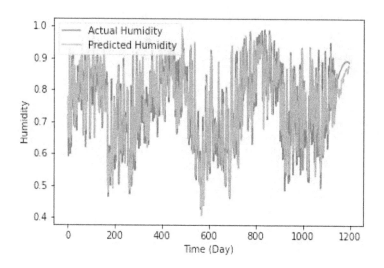

Figure 5.6: Graphical analysis of actual v/s predicted Humidity for CRNN model

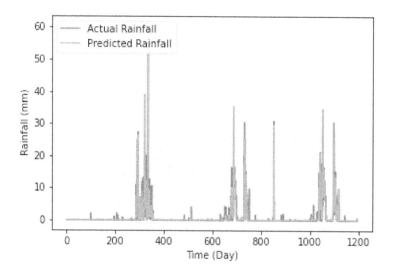

Figure 5.7: Graphical analysis of actual v/s predicted Rainfall for CRNN model

The graphs below in Figure 5.8, Figure 5.9, Figure 5.10 and Figure 5.11 gives the values of performance metrics on various epochs for temperature, wind speed, humidity and rainfall in which the x-axis is the epoch range and the y-axis is the values of metrics.

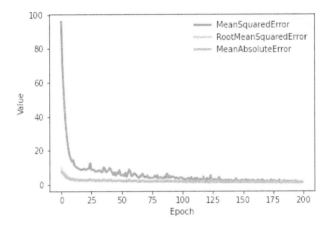

Figure 5.8: Performance metrics at various epoch for Temperature

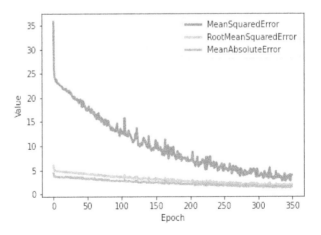

Figure 5.9: Performance metrics at various epoch for Wind Speed

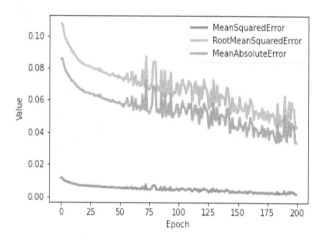

Figure 5.10: Performance metrics at various epoch for Humidity

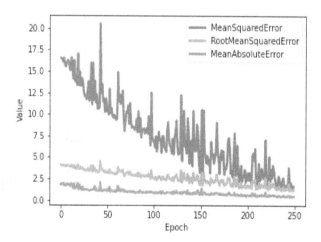

Figure 5.11: Performance metrics at various epoch for Rainfall

The least MSE is found at the 177 epochs for temperature, 340 epochs for wind speed, 198 epochs for humidity and 236 epochs for rainfall parameter

CHAPTER-6

WEATHER FORECASTING USING PROPOSED HYBRID_STACKED BI-LSTM

Chapter 6

Weather Forecasting using Proposed Hybrid_Stacked Bi-LSTM

6.1 Hybrid_Stacked Bi-LSTM Model

The proposed Hybrid_Stacked Bi-LSTM deep learning model discussed in this chapter is a combination of LSTM and Bi-LSTM learning and training models. The versatility and non-linear adaptive processing ability of neural networks make them very useful for prediction.

Generally, the basis for the prediction of effective short-term weather forecasting is to use the previous several time steps along with the dependencies between time series, which cannot be achieved by traditional neural networks. A RNN is typically used to infer future events using historical data. For the evaluation of the network performance, gradient descent method is generally used for the training of neural networks, but Back Propagation Through Time (BPTT) is the training algorithm used in the traditional RNN. As a result, if training time is increased beyond a limit, then the returned residual of the network will reduce exponentially and hence the renewal of network weights will be slow down. Therefore, in practical applications, the traditional RNN exhibits vanishing gradients, which means that a memory block is necessary to embody the effect of long-term memory and as described in Section 2.2 and 2.2.4. Unlike the LSTM, the Bi-LSTM is having two layers, out of which one layer conducts operations in the forward direction of the data sequence (time-series data), and the second layer performs operations in the reverse direction of the data sequence. Therefore, the LSTM is combined with the Bi-LSTM and the other reason is that; the number of neurons does not have any relationship with the length of sequences in the LSTM model. However, the LSTM model seems to meet the real time requirements, but not capable to handle the accuracy requirement for the prediction of weather forecasting. Therefore, a special type of RNN namely Hybrid_Stacked Bi-LSTM neural network is proposed, which is based on the LSTM and Bi-LSTM model and is capable of maintaining long-term dependencies and read any length of sequence, assuming that the hybrid model provides better prediction.

The network structure and parameters of Hybrid_Stacked Bi-LSTM is optimized experimentally in order to maintain different weather conditions, so that the above two requirements can be satisfied at the same time with the proposed model for the prediction of weather forecasting.

6.2 Forecasting Approach in Hybrid_Stacked Bi-LSTM

A hybrid stacked LSTM and Bi-LSTM neural network structure (Hybrid_Stacked Bi-LSTM) is proposed in the work to improve the accuracy of weather prediction. Figure 6.1 depicts the proposed deep learning model with stacked LSTM and Bi-LSTM layers for the MISO model.

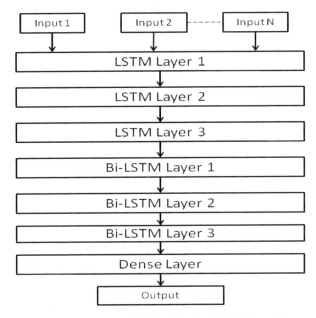

Figure 6.1: Proposed Hybrid_Stacked Bi-LSTM model

The proposed Hybrid_Stacked Bi-LSTM neural network structure consists of three stacked LSTM layers and three stacked Bi-LSTM layers as part of overall composition known as nodes. These nodes utilize a set of coefficients to carry out computational operations using a combination of data and input. With the experimental observations, the number of layers and memory cells in each layer are determined for the best performance. By integrating memory units, these models may learn long-term dependencies. These memory units allow the network to acquire new information, forget previously hidden states, and update previously hidden states.

The overall structure consists of an Input Layer, three stacked LSTM layers of 256, 128, 64 units respectively, three stacked Bi-LSTM layers of 32, 16, 8 units respectively, one dense layer of unit 8 and one output layer. An issue with LSTMs and Bi-LSTMs is that they can easily over fit training data, reducing their predictive skill so to handle this dropout layer is also incorporated for every LSTM and Bi-LSTM layer with value of 0.2 for reducing over fitting and improving model performance. To optimize our model, 'Adam' is used as optimizer. Larger datasets are used to train LSTM models and this process often requires multiple days even with the Graphical Processing Unit.

The proposed model is a multiple input single output regression model which takes multiple input parameters and gives a single parameter as output. The reason behind the selection of multiple input single output regression models is described in section 3.2. As discussed in Section 3.1, seven surface weather parameters are fed into the network as inputs for this model variance and is expected to predict a single appropriate parameter as the output. In this approach, four different models are required for weather forecasting as all of them are trained so as to predict a particular weather parameter.

LSTM layer

Long Short Term Memory (LSTM) is a type of recurrent neural network that finds its use in time series applications such as speech recognition, text recognition and language modeling [275] since it assimilates long-term dependencies. It is an appropriate method for prediction because it contains memory cell units to remember long time state values of sequential data, the gate units to learn the relevant state to retain and utilize [276]. It is preferable for the above-mentioned applications due to its ability to handle unstructured data and also structured data with a non-linear pattern. To the best of our knowledge, only a few attempts have been made using LSTM[277], especially in rainfall prediction[278]. Hence an attempt is made in our research with a novel approach.

95

LSTM is a variant of Recurrent Neural Networks. RNNs are special types of Neural Networks with recurring properties. It takes current input example, and what they have perceived previously in time as their input as well. Based on RNN structure, LSTM adds three gate functions: input, forgetting, and output gates, which regulate the input, memory, and output values, respectively. Neural networks normally function like a black box where the decisions are made based on given inputs. It uses static memory in the form of weights to store information about learning experiences. In order to provide explicit representation for memory in RNNs, the LSTM network was introduced. The memory unit is described as 'cell' in the network and these models are adaptation of RNN's and are best suited for sequential data. In this proposed research, we want to investigate the effectiveness of LSTM for weather forecasting. The structure of LSTM network used for this research is given in Figure 6.2

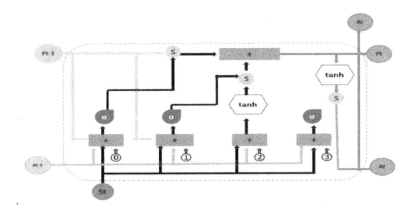

Figure 6.2: Structure of a LSTM network

According to above Figure 6.2, the LSTM network takes three inputs at, 'S$_t$', 'A$_{t-1}$', 'P$_{t-1}$'. 'S$_t$' is the input vector for the current time step. 'A$_{t-1}$' is the output or hidden state transferred by the previous LSTM unit. And 'P$_{t-1}$' is the memory element or cell state of the previous unit. It has two outputs such as, 'A$_t$' and 'P$_t$', where, 'A$_t$' is the output of the current unit and 'Pt' is the memory element of the current unit. Every decision is made after considering current input, previous output and previous memory information. When the current output is obtained the memory is updated. The 'S' indicates the 'Forget' element of multiplication. When the value of the forget element is given as '0' it forgets ninety percent of old memory. For all other values such as 1, 2, and 3, a fraction of old memory is allowed by the unit. The plus operator is present for the piece wise summation to summarize old and new memory. The amount of old memory is decided by the 'S' sign. As a result of two operations, P_{t-1} is changed to P_t. The activation functions described in the Figure 6.2 are the sigmoid and tanh activation functions having output as a forget valves. The second activation valve is termed as a new memory element as it includes old memory while processing new inputs. The old memory, previous output and current input along with a bias vector decides the amount of memory to be given as input to the next unit.

LSTM is made of three gates, such as Input gate, Forget gate and Output gate. These are specified by the activation function 'sigmoid' in the range of '0' to '1'where, '0' blocks all data from entering and '1' does the direct opposite. The function is expected to produce a positive output which gives the accurate result.

$$i_t = \sigma \left(w_i \left[A_{t-1}, S_t \right] + b_i \right) \tag{6.1}$$

$$f_t = \sigma \left(w_f \left[A_{t-1}, S_t \right] + b_f \right) \tag{6.2}$$

$$o_t = \sigma \left(w_t \left[A_{t-1}, S_t \right] + b_t \right) \tag{6.3}$$

In above equations, LHS denote input, forget and output gates by variables 'i', 'f' and 'o'. Sigma (σ) represents the activation function sigmoid. 'w' denotes the weights assigned to the neurons present in the respective gates. 'A_{t-1}'denotes the hidden state of the previous unit at time t-1. 'S_t' is the input of the current time step. 'b' denotes the biases for the three gates as 0, 1, 2 and 3. Further, equation 6.1 specifies the nature of information to be carried forward by the input gate. Equation 6.2 denotes the amount of past information from the previous unit to be forgotten by the current unit. Equation 6.3 provides activation to the output gate for the current time step.

$$\tilde{C}_t = \tanh(w_c[A_{t-1},S_t]+b_c) \tag{6.4}$$

$$C_t = f_t * C_{t-1} + i_t * \tilde{C}_t \tag{6.5}$$

$$A_t = o_t * \tanh(C_t) \tag{6.6}$$

C_t is the memory information for the current time step and $\tilde{C}_t$ denotes the candidate for the present cell state. The symbol '*' indicates the multiplication of given vectors element wise.

From the equations 6.4, 6.5 and 6.6, it is clear that, for the given past memory, the nature of information to forget and the final output is derived using activation function in equation 6.6.

By switching between the input and forget gates, the LSTM can selectively consider its current inputs or forget its previous memory. The output gate, meanwhile, learns how much memory cell must be transferred to the hidden state. With these additional memory cells, the LSTM can learn extremely complicated and long-term temporal dynamics.

LSTMs have typically been criticized for the large number of components whose function is not clear yet. In addition, LSTMs are prone to consuming a set of memory to store partial results for their multiple cell gates, especially when the input sequence is long. This is the case for the time-series weather data. For the reason, Hybrid architecture has been explored to model and predict fine-grained weather data.

Bi-LSTM Layer

Bi-directional LSTM has taken considerable attraction from its initial introduction in 2001 for time series data [240]. Similar to the LSTM, the Bi-LSTM can be used for multiple input single output models. In LSTM, data are preserved from inputs that have already passed through its hidden state (i.e. the LSTM only preserves the past information). In contrast, as described in Section 2.4.4, the Bi-LSTM networks will run inputs in two ways, namely from the past to the future and from the future to the past. That is, the Bi-LSTM can run the inputs backwards to preserve information from the future compared to the LSTM networks[241][242][243]. Therefore, the Bi-LSTM can preserve both past and future information using the two hidden states combined. This process is helped by Bi-LSTM to better understand the context and thus targets a more accurate forecast compared to the LSTM networks when it is combined with LSTM in sequence-to-sequence applications (i.e. it knows the full inputs at prediction time)[244]. Figure 6.3 depicts the basic structure of a Bi-LSTM.

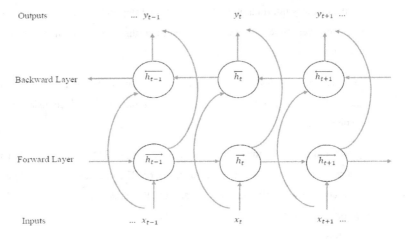

Figure 6.3: Structure of a Bi-LSTM network.

As presented in Figure 6.3, Bi-LSTM processes data in both directions with two separate hidden layers. The processed results are sent to the output layer. Equation 6.7 and Equation 6.8 represent the calculation of hidden vector sequence h = (h₁, h₂, . . ., hₜ) and output vector sequence y = (y₁, y₂, . . . ,y_T) based on input sequence x = (x₁, x₂, . . . , x_T) in conventional RNN [242].

$$h_t = \mathcal{H}(W_{xh}x_t + W_{hh}h_{t-1} + b_n) \qquad (6.7)$$

$$y_t = W_{hy}h_t + b_y \qquad (6.8)$$

Notations of the Equation 6.7 and 6.8 are: W- weight matrices (for example W_{xh} is the input-hidden weight matrix); b- bias vector; $\mathcal{H}$- hidden layer function.

Deep Bi-LSTM networks refer to stacking multiple Bi-LSTM hidden layers on top of each other to establish a network. Bi-LSTM can produce a better prediction for the time series data when it is combined with the LSTM due to two-way data preservation [262][279]. The only drawback of these networks is that they are less efficient for training, testing, and predicting data compared to the LSTM (i.e. Bi-LSTM has taken time to train models and testing) [243]. As per section 2.5, it is evident that there has been no attempt taken to experiment with the combination of LSTM and Bi-LSTM for weather forecasting in the literature.

Proposed Hybrid_Stacked Bi-LSTM Deep learning model is evaluated with several configurations and controls to find an optimal model with least MSE. Each network configuration has a different number of layers and each layer consists of a different number of nodes. These configurations have experimented with different controls mainly learning rate and optimizer. The model gives the best value with Adam optimizer, batch size 32 and learning rate 0.01. MSE cost function is selected to find the loss for experiments as this study is based on regression modelling, which is calculated as Equation 3.3. The least MSE is found at the 177 epochs for temperature, 345 epochs for wind speed, 179 epochs for humidity and 243 for rainfall parameter.

The other obvious hyper parameter is data_dim=7 (i.e. the number of parameters in each timeslot), time steps=30, the shape of the training dataset (2792, 30, 7) where 2792 is the number of samples in the training dataset followed by time steps and data_dim.

LSTM and Bi-LSTM network with same configuration and controls individually generated predicted values but with lower accuracy for all the four parameters. It drove the way forward for the designing of hybrid model assuming that Hybrid_Stacked Bi-LSTM model improves the prediction results.

6.3 Results

As described in Section 3.1, the proposed Hybrid_Stacked Bi-LSTM model is trained with the training dataset and testing dataset is used to get a prediction using the trained model. The prediction results are compared with the ground truth for all four parameters. As described in Section 6.2, the model is evaluated with several configurations and controls to find an optimal model with least MSE and 'save the best model' approach is used while training the model. In this case, the system checks the loss function value for each epoch with the saved model. Only if the new loss value was smaller than the saved model loss, the system saved the new model as the best model. The saved best model is used to get the prediction for the testing dataset and evaluate the results with respect to the ground truth. The model is evaluated mainly using the MSE metric. While evaluating the results, there are some other metrics also employed such as MAE, RMSE. All of these evaluation metrics work in a similar manner to calculate the error. The values of these errors should be minimum for better performance of the model. In a practical situation, the values of some weather parameters can be zero. Some examples are rain and even temperature. This is one of the main reasons the regression modelling prefers to use averages to calculate the errors, such as MSE, MAE, and RMSE.

Table 6.1 presents the best MSE, RMSE and MAE values for all four parameters for Hybrid_Stacked Bi-LSTM. Table 6.2 and Table 6.3 present the values for all four parameters for LSTM and Bi-LSTM respectively. This evaluation is carried out using the actual values and not the normalized data (i.e. the normalized predictions are converted to the human-understandable form and compared with the actual ground truth values).

Table 6.1: Evaluation results for Hybrid_Stacked Bi-LSTM model

Parameters	Evaluation Metrics		
	MSE	RMSE	MAE
Temperature	0.486	0.697	0.517
Wind Speed	0.856	0.925	0.677
Humidity	0.0002	0.0155	0.0119
Rainfall	0.763	0.873	0.290

Table 6.2: Evaluation results for LSTM model

Parameters	Evaluation Metrics		
	MSE	RMSE	MAE
Temperature	0.839	0.916	0.703
Wind Speed	1.051	1.025	0.688
Humidity	0.0009	0.0312	0.0243
Rainfall	0.977	0.988	0.407

Table 6.3: Evaluation results for Bi-LSTM model

Parameters	Evaluation Metrics		
	MSE	RMSE	MAE
Temperature	1.355	1.164	0.876
Wind Speed	2.357	1.535	1.185
Humidity	0.0010	0.0321	0.0246
Rainfall	1.939	1.392	0.525

The values of all these evaluation metrics for the proposed Hybrid_Stacked Bi-LSTM model are given in Table 6.1. It shows the skills of the proposed model for forecasting future weather data which gives best results for all parameters when it is compared to the results of LSTM given in Table 6.2 and Bi-LSTM given in Table 6.3. Hence, it is evident from the result that LSTM and Bi-LSTM model can be combined for more efficient result for weather forecasting.

As there are 1197 samples in testing data, the Hybrid_Stacked Bi-LSTM model will produce a similar number of outputs as the predicted data. It is difficult to visualize all of these predictions because of the large sample size so the prediction results of all four parameters for the 1197 days are presented graphically. Figure 6.4, Figure 6.5, Figure 6.6 and Figure 6.7 displays the prediction result of temperature, wind speed, humidity and rainfall respectively where the blue line represents the ground truth (Actual) values for the particular day while orange line represents the prediction results for the corresponding day.

The prediction results will be compared with the results of other models in Chapter 7 to determine the accuracy and suitability of the model.

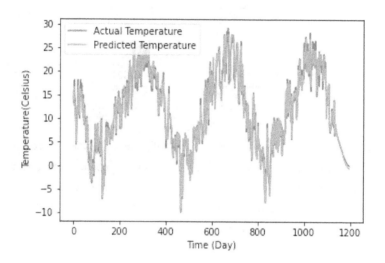

Figure 6.4: Graphical analysis of actual v/s predicted Temperature for Hybrid_Stacked Bi-LSTM model

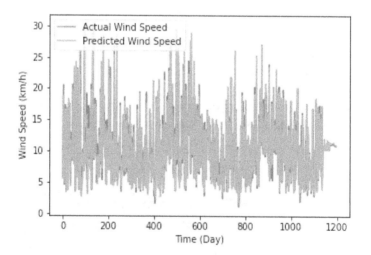

Figure 6.5: Graphical analysis of actual v/s predicted Wind Speed for Hybrid_Stacked Bi-LSTM model

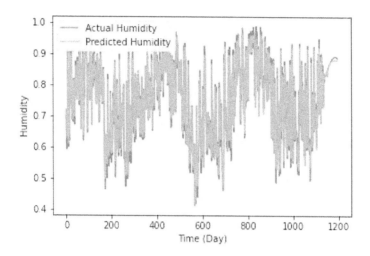

Figure 6.6: Graphical analysis of actual v/s predicted Humidity for Hybrid_Stacked

Bi-LSTM model

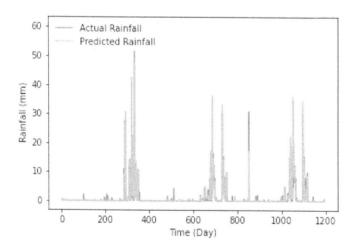

Figure 6.7: Graphical analysis of actual v/s predicted Rainfall for Hybrid_Stacked

Bi-LSTM model

The graphs below in Figure 6.8, Figure 6.9, Figure 6.10 and Figure 6.11 gives the values of performance metrics on various epochs for temperature, wind speed, humidity and rainfall in which the x-axis is the epoch range and the y-axis is the values of metrics.

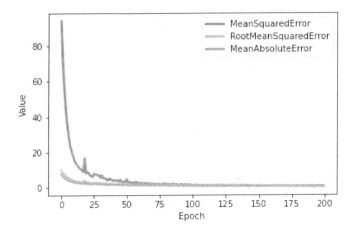

Figure 6.8: Performance metrics at various epoch for Temperature

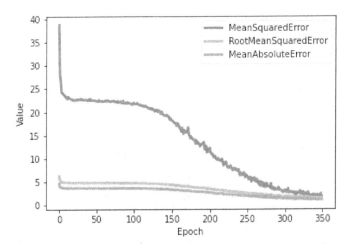

Figure 6.9: Performance metrics at various epoch for Wind Speed

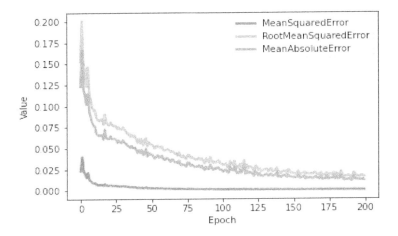

Figure 6.10: Performance metrics at various epoch for Humidity

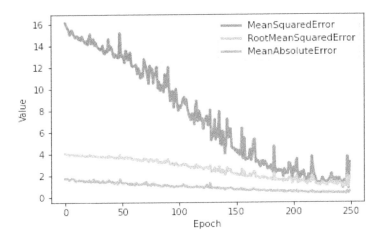

Figure 6.11: Performance metrics at various epoch for Rainfall

The least MSE is found at 177 epochs for temperature, 345 epochs for wind speed, 179 epochs for humidity and 243 epochs for rainfall parameter.

CHAPTER-7

ANALYSIS AND

DISCUSSIONS

Chapter 7

Analysis and Discussions

In this chapter, the performance of the proposed Hybrid_Stacked Bi-LSTM discussed in chapter 6 is compared with the well-established statistical Model ARIMA discussed in chapter 4 and deep learning model CRNN discussed in chapter 5. As described in sections 3.3, these models are evaluated using multiple input single output regression type for all four parameters and the performance metrics used are MSE, RMSE and MAE as describe in section 3.4.Additionally, the above experiments are successful means that the proposed deep learning model can be utilized for forecasting the weather.

Table 7.1: Comparison of various models for Temperature forecasting

Models	MSE	RMSE	MAE
ARIMA	2.252	1.500	0.806
CRNN	1.368	1.169	0.890
Hybrid_Stacked Bi-LSTM	0.486	0.697	0.517

Table 7.1 gives comparative analysis of performance of ARIMA, CRNN and Proposed Hybrid_Stacked Bi-LSTM models for temperature forecasting on different metrics and Figure 7.1 shows graphical analysis of MSE, RMSE and MAE respectively.

Table 7.2: Comparison of various models for Wind Speed forecasting

Models	MSE	RMSE	MAE
ARIMA	4.964	2.228	1.700
CRNN	2.706	1.645	1.256
Hybrid_Stacked Bi-LSTM	0.856	0.925	0.677

Table 7.2 gives comparative analysis of performance of ARIMA, CRNN and Proposed Hybrid_Stacked Bi-LSTM models for wind speed forecasting on different metrics and Figure 7.2 shows graphical analysis of MSE, RMSE and MAE respectively.

Table 7.3: Comparison of various models for Humidity forecasting

Models	MSE	RMSE	MAE
ARIMA	0.0030	0.0551	0.0446
CRNN	0.0018	0.0428	0.0341
Hybrid_Stacked Bi-LSTM	0.0002	0.0155	0.0119

Table 7.3 gives comparative analysis of performance of ARIMA, CRNN and Proposed Hybrid_Stacked Bi-LSTM models for humidity forecasting on different metrics and Figure 7.3 shows graphical analysis of MSE, RMSE and MAE respectively.

Table 7.4: Comparison of various models for Rainfall forecasting

Models	MSE	RMSE	MAE
ARIMA	3.753	1.937	0.755
CRNN	1.369	1.170	0.469
Hybrid_Stacked Bi-LSTM	0.763	0.873	0.209

Table 7.4 gives comparative analysis of performance of ARIMA, CRNN and Proposed Hybrid_Stacked Bi-LSTM models for rainfall forecasting on different metrics and Figure 7.4 shows graphical analysis of MSE, RMSE and MAE respectively.

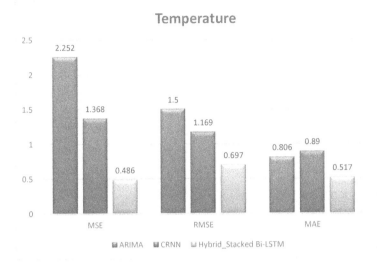

Figure 7.1: Evaluation metrics for Temperature

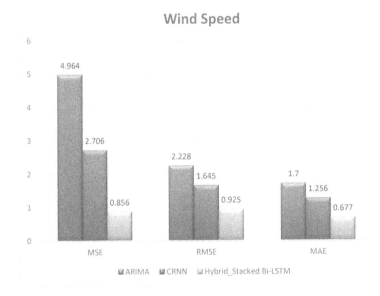

Figure 7.2: Evaluation metrics for Wind Speed

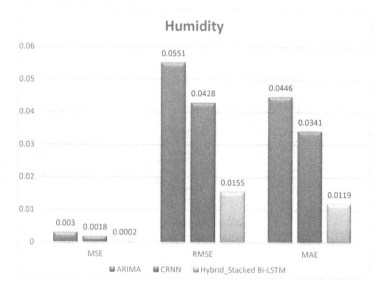

Figure 7.3: Evaluation metrics for Humidity

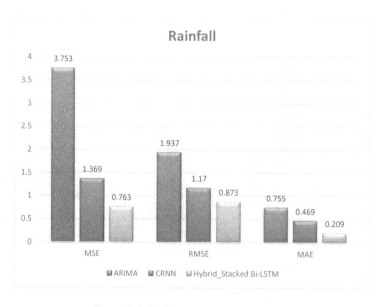

Figure 7.4: Evaluation metrics for Rainfall

Discussion

As discussed in Section 2.5, there has been no previous attempt to combine deep learning models LSTM and Bi-directional LSTM for weather prediction. This study has significantly advanced the current knowledge by combining the above two models. From the results of this study, it is apparent that the AI-based deep learning Hybrid_Stacked Bi-LSTM model, can give more accurate forecast when it is compared to the statistical model ARIMA and deep learning model CRNN. This is also proved that deep learning models have a high degree of accuracy in capturing non-linear or complicated underlying properties of a physical process. Besides, Section 2.3 demonstrates that there are various challenges in the NWP models including that use of high computing power to execute a large number of non-linear simultaneous equations, and it requires a long time for processing. As Section 6.2 discussed, the proposed model can overcome these computational complexity issues. This also validates the statement in Section 2.3 that the computing power of NWP methods can be reduced by using data-driven computer modelling methods.

As described in Section 2.5, there is a knowledge gap which has been little or no attempt to compare statistical approaches with a cutting-edge deep neural network approach for weather forecasting. This study compared statistical approach ARIMA and deep learning model CRNN with combined deep learning approaches of LSTM and Bi-Directional LSTM for historical weather data with MISO regression models. As shown in Table 7.1, Table 7.2, Table 7.3 and Table 7.4, it is evidenced that the proposed deep learning Hybrid_Stacked Bi-LSTM model performed significantly better than the statistical model ARIMA and deep learning model CRNN for all four parameters.

As per information from Table 2.2 in Section 2.4, the existing AI-based weather forecasting models used only five or less interrelated input parameters. Besides, an absolute AI-based weather forecasting model has not been explored yet. This study significantly contributes to the current knowledge by exploring a complete AI-based weather forecasting model with seven parameters as input. Even, comparative analysis of this research demonstrates that the proposed model can be used for fine-grained area-specific weather forecasting for the community of users in a specific geographical area. As a result, the suggested approach has the potential to have a substantial impact on a community of users who rely on the weather for their day to day activities. For example, the weather condition can be predicted and monitored by the proposed model, without relying on the regional weather forecasting. The only requirement is to access the local weather station data, which could be achieved by setting up an economical weather station in specific locations or farms. Furthermore, a broader set of users who rely on favourable weather conditions could get the advantage of the model, such as places of interest, schools, outdoor sports centres, construction sites, etc

CHAPTER-8

CONCLUSION AND

FUTURE WORK

Chapter 8

Conclusion and Future Work

8.1 Conclusion

The overall goal of this study is to obtain an effective and fine-grained weather forecasting model for a community of users in a specific geographical area. This research demonstrates that the proposed Hybrid_Stacked Bi-LSTM model for the historical weather data can be used for the forecasting of weather. The model has outperformed the statistical model ARIMA and deep learning model CRNN in all four parameters. The proposed model is able to run on a standalone computer and it can be easily deployed in a selected geographical region for fine-grained weather prediction. For instance, the proposed model could be deployed using a low-cost and low-power device. Besides, the proposed model is able to overcome several challenges of existing models such as the understanding of the model, its installation, and its execution and portability. In particular, the deep model is portable and can be easily installed in a Python environment for effective results. This process is highly efficient compared to the existing NWP models. The existing NWP models are limited to regional forecasting. Besides, the existing machine learning-based weather forecasting models are limited to predict limited weather parameters. The proposed new weather forecasting model can predict as many as four parameters. The experiment results show that this deep neural network approach can be applied for weather prediction. Consequently, this new model could make a significant impact on a community of users who rely on the weather for their day-to-day activities.

The proposed model has advantages over the regional and global forecasting models including lower computational power consumption, ease of installation, and greater portability. While the NWP models are viable for long-range forecast and not for a fine-grained geographical area, the proposed model could make a reliable and accurate prediction as this uses the data related to that specific location.

8.2 Limitations and Recommendations

This research is carried out using seven different surface weather parameters. An increased number of inputs would probably lead to enhanced results. However, this will increase the model complexity requiring a large number of parameters to estimate. Furthermore, seventy percent of total weather data of only 2792 days are used to train the proposed model. Increasing the size of the training data sample could result in better prediction of a deep learning network. The created model can be fine-tuned with more data to get better performance. There could be a possibility to improve the prediction by introducing some more weather parameters such as soil temperature, soil moisture, snow, solar radiation balance, and pressure at different levels.

Besides, the MISO approach is utilized within this research for the prediction of weather conditions which produces better MSE values when it is compared with MIMO; even though this method is less efficient then MIMO. Therefore, there is a huge potential the MIMO approach will increase the accuracy of the results. Moreover, the Bi-LSTM yields high accuracy, long-term prediction when combined with LSTM as discussed in section 2.4.4. Therefore, more accurate results could be generated by the more efficient use of Bi-LSTM; even if this method is not efficient due to the high time-consumption.

In addition to the above recommendations, there are some limitations to this research as well. The training process of the deep model is complex as there are several configurations and controls to manage and the time consumption is increased for training depending on the size of the dataset. There are some controls kept constant during the training process. Besides, there are some control experiments with limited possibilities (For example, Adam and RMSProp are the only optimizer experiments with deep learning models among many alternatives). There could be a possibility to improve the prediction results if the experiment uses constant controls as variables or controls with many different options. Again, each of these experiments consumes comparatively a long time for completion. As a solution, there could be a possibility to use high specification hardware resources to train the models (For instance, 24 GB GPU memory with 16 core CPU and 32 GB RAM). On the contrary, these training experiments are carried out at once and the trained model is used for prediction. The prediction process is neither complex nor time-consuming. Therefore, it is fairly unsought to only spend excessively on high specific hardware for the training process. The other main limitation is that the practical difficulties in selecting appropriate parameters for weather prediction. As there are many weather parameters, it is not practically possible to classify in such a way as to identify a subset of parameters for the machine learning models. It is practically impossible to calculate the impact of removing or fixing a subset of input parameters on the generated model output. The other limitation is that the deep learning models prefer larger datasets to train models targeting accurate prediction. The training complexity is increased when increasing the size of the training dataset.

8.3 Reflection and Future Work

According to the results of this research, it is apparent that the proposed deep neural network is able to produce accurate and fine-grained weather forecasting results. This study has hugely contributed to the knowledge by accomplishing the main contribution and other contributions as described in Section 1.5. Furthermore, a wider set of users who rely on favorable weather conditions could get the advantage of the model such as farms, places of interest, schools, outdoor sports centers, and larger construction sites.

This research initially targeted on developing a fine-grained weather forecasting model. However, there could be a different way to carry out this research to achieve both regional and fine-grained forecasting by connecting data from different weather stations in different geographical areas. The selected weather station data can be used for fine-grained forecast while a combination of different weather stations data could be used to regional forecast.

Besides, the WRF model produces better forecasting results on a very long-term basis compared to the deep learning model. The reason is that the WRF model is combined with many other climate models [280][281] and data are globally entered as input into the system. The proposed lightweight fine-grained weather forecasting model could be combined with the existing climate model targeting a more accurate and long-term weather forecast. In the meantime, it is praiseworthy to consider combining the local weather station data to regional weather data. This could increase the accuracy of the proposed model.

Therefore, the future studies of this research include; combining different local weather station data for a regional level forecast, combining the existing climate models to the proposed forecasting model, and combining local and regional weather forecast data for an accurate and fine-grained weather model.

CPSIA information can be obtained
at www.ICGtesting.com
Printed in the USA
LVHW020649250423
745210LV00009B/406